BIEBER

LIFE IN
THE LOOP

ESSAYS ON
OCD

MATT
BIEBER

LIFE IN
THE LOOP

ESSAYS
ON OCD

CONTENTS

THE FIRST FEW CHAPTERS

OF A LIFE WITH OCD

PREFACE

Just as the infernal forest of razor leaves, just as the winged creatures from hell are really brought into being by my actions....

-ŚĀNTIDEVA, BODHICARYĀVATĀRA

When I was 18, I was diagnosed with obsessive-compulsive disorder (OCD). Since then, I've occasionally considered writing about my experiences, but I've tended not to trust my motives. Writing about my experiences, I thought, would be a way to redeem them, to justify an early adulthood that hadn't measured up to my adolescent hopes and dreams. I may not have been happy in my twenties, I thought, but at least I'd have a book – and perhaps the beginning of a writing career – to show for it.

It was a cracked notion, of course. I was so caught up in the grip of OCD – and in my flight from it – that I could never have written about those experiences. I didn't want to spend any more time with them, didn't want to be anywhere near them.

But at some level, I felt like I was owed. I've had to suffer day in and day out for years. Maybe I can cash in on that suffering. This didn't feel like the noblest of impulses, of course, but I was floundering: what else was I going to do with myself? I was in my mid-20s, moving around a lot and working a series of jobs that didn't mean much to me. I hadn't found much direction, and when I looked, OCD was usually in the way.

As I came to see, however, the idea of cashing in on my suffering was itself compulsive – a way to feed an insatiable feeling of insufficiency, to measure up to some external (and endlessly receding) standard. I didn't want to write a book because of what it might teach me or what it might allow me to express. I wanted to write a book because I suspected that lurid stories of suffering would sell, and because I couldn't imagine how else to feel good about myself. When I saw this – that my desire to write was itself a product of OCD – I decided to treat it that way and did my best not to give in.

More recently, though, things have shifted. I feel less and less of a need to apologize to the world (or to myself) for the way my life has unfolded. And as I've begun to feel freer to live this life – as opposed to something more grandiose – I've also begun to feel more capable of spending time thinking about some of my more painful experiences.

These new forms of resilience have many roots. Some of them – including six years of intensive cognitive behavioral therapy, as well as an exposure to Buddhism and the beginnings of a meditation practice – are quite specific. Others feel like more general products of growing up and listening to the lessons of my life.

The upshot is that I've begun exploring my OCD in a public-facing way. I started by making a series of videos entitled "What OCD is Like" and publishing them on my blog. (There are six in total; they're available at www.mattbieber.net).

As the series title indicates, these videos focus mostly on the phenomenology of OCD – what it feels like to undergo an often-constant assault of painful, intrusive thoughts. When I made the videos, I didn't feel comfortable prescribing anything, musing about the meanings of mental illness, or delving into contemporary neuro-psychological research. Instead, I simply tried to relate what it feels like to have a brain that works the way mine does.

Making these videos was surprisingly gratifying, and more gratifying still were the responses I received. Every now and again, I would receive a blog comment or an e-mail in which someone thanked me for sharing my experiences. Often, my correspondents would offer up deeply personal experiences of their own. I didn't have a word for it at the time, but looking back, these dialogues were the beginnings of what felt like a mutual ministry.

The work you have in your hands represents something slightly more ambitious. In the pages that follow, I attempt to weave my first several years of experience with OCD into the larger story of my life. In doing so, I hope to provide myself a bit more coherence about where I've come from and where I might be headed.

Just as importantly, I hope to offer up a raw and naked account of a disease that is too often trivialized or misunderstood. I want to share something that others can relate to – both OCD sufferers and those who simply wish to understand more about this condition.

Along the way, I'm going to describe some episodes in graphic detail. When I do so, I will always strive to keep my eye on the true and the useful. Our lives are far too precious for me to waste yours by rendering mine as some exotic grotesque.

One open question for me has to do with the therapeutic value of writing works like this (or reading them, for that matter). As my thesis advisor, the anthropologist Michael Jackson, has pointed out, our culture places a great deal of faith in the power of storytelling to untie mental knots. Sometimes, however, that faith is misplaced, and OCD can be one such venue. I have described my experiences hundreds of times to friends and family, often at the risk of re-living those experiences. On occasion, doing so has helped me escape my own dimly lit inner chambers, connect to the people I love, and enjoy momentarily relief.

Many times, however, sharing in this way has functioned as a trap, a covert way to seek reassurance by tracking down evidence that my worries are ill-founded. Seeking reassurance in this way is deeply counterproductive for OCD sufferers; doing so exacerbates tormenting feelings, strengthens obsessive and compulsive patterns, and undermines successful therapy.

All that is to say, then, that I'm not entirely sure what the effects of this writing will be on my efforts to deal with OCD. Still, I do have a deep faith that changing the way I experience the world depends on scrutinizing how my consciousness works in the here and now. This means creating situations in which I can replay my experiences without feeling drawn in or taken over. Thankfully, writing has often proved a good medium for doing so – a way of creating just enough distance from the howling maw to see things a little more clearly.

Of course, this doesn't mean that I look forward to reliving the experiences I will describe. But I'm not sure I see any alternative. Creating change has to begin by reckoning with what is.

One last note: at the outset of this work, Professor Jackson gave me a great piece of advice. Write the chronology first, he said. Get the whole story down, the full sequence of events, from OCD's first appearance to your latest efforts at therapy. Then, separately, record your reflections on these experiences – the philosophical, theological, and poetic self-inquiry that will show readers how you've come to understand what you've gone through.

It was excellent counsel, I thought, and I would have followed it if I could. But as I've discovered, I don't know how to keep events distinct from my thoughts *about* the events. In one sense, this dilemma encapsulates OCD itself (or at least my variety of OCD): the thoughts – and a certain way of responding to them – *are* the disease. Exploring the implications of this truth will form a significant portion of what follows.

CHAPTER ONE

"But," we might ask, "if our real condition is an awakened state, why are we so busy trying to avoid becoming aware of it?" It is because we have become so absorbed in our confused view of the world, that we consider it real, the only possible world.

-CHÖGYAM TRUNGPA, *CUTTING THROUGH SPIRITUAL MATERIALISM*

When I was a boy, my mother would tuck me in bed each night. Sometimes, she would return to her knitting or paperwork. Other times, however, she would go around the house, checking each of the closets for burglars. After she had checked all the closets, she would check them again. And again. And maybe one final time.

This isn't going to be about blame. For a long time, parts of me wished it could be – that I could just lay all of my guilt and frustration at Mom's feet and say, "I'm like this because this is what you showed me, because this is how you taught me to understand myself." But of course, the next clause would be, "Because you are like this." I wanted it to be her free will that could have averted all of this, if only she had exercised it properly. I wanted her to be responsible.

The trouble with that line of thinking, of course, is that blame and responsibility go together. If I'm off the hook, then so is she.

Beginning in high school, I spent a lot of time arguing with my friends and myself about free will and determinism. I suspected that most people are overly invested in the idea that they have control over the choices that they make, and that choices themselves were a kind of illusion, a disguised wish to believe that we are in charge of our lives.

My friend E would ask me what I was talking about. "Look, I'm eating a candy bar," he'd say. "I could have chosen *not* to eat this candy bar." And in one sense, he was right. It was easy to imagine things having gone the other way. There was no visible obstacle, nothing we could see that would have prevented him from choosing licorice or ice cream instead.

But that wasn't enough. Yes, we could *imagine* things having gone differently. But imagining things didn't make them possible. After all, the moment in which E reached for the candy bar didn't just happen. Rather, a whole set of forces, an entire history, had led up to that moment. For something different to happen, wouldn't history itself have to have gone differently?

In college, the work of the philosopher Peter van Inwagen helped me find voice for these intuitions. According to van Inwagen, it wasn't enough to imagine a world in which E had left the candy bar uneaten. Rather, we had to go further, to imagine how an alternative choice would have been made. And to do that, we had to trace history backwards, to find the point at which the decision had occurred, in which factors had been weighed and an outcome calculated. Some of that history was easy to track down – *I want the candy bar; I'm hungry; I saw this advertisement for Snickers bars last week.* But the closer we looked for the actual decisive moment – and the more I looked for these kinds of moments in my own life – the more elusive they seemed. Yes, I could relate to moments in which options presented themselves. And yes, I could even relate to moments in which some of them were eliminated, in which I found myself embarking on some course of action. What I couldn't relate to was the sense that I had any control over what took place in those moments. They just seemed to happen. There were options, and then there weren't.

It felt just like remembering a phone number (or anything else, for that matter). You could try to jog your memory – cycling through associations or sequences of events – but the moment in which the memory actually appeared was always mysterious. It simply arose out of the murky black, without passport or stamp.

Each summer growing up, my mom and step-dad and I went to the beach for a couple of weeks with another family. We would get up early on a Sunday morning and drive the six or seven hours to Southern Shores, North Carolina, a small town on the Outer Banks. Many years, our first stop was a restaurant called The Black Pelican.

It was the kind of restaurant that makes kids feel like they're getting one over on their parents – *How did we talk them into this?* For us kids, it was crab legs by the pound and pizzas with fancy cheeses. But our parents liked the place too – there were oysters and Bloody Marys and a view out onto the sand dunes. The rustic, fisherman's house atmosphere didn't seem overdone like so many of the places down the beach, and we all had our own ways of loving it. (The men's' bathroom also gave us boys and our dads one more thing to agree on, if ever so obliquely: just above the urinals was an artsy photograph of a naked woman rising up on her belly from beneath impossibly white sheets.)

The restaurant also had a t-shirt shop, something I now find tacky but at the time found almost overwhelmingly cool. During one of our visits, everyone in the group decided to get one. I had a difficult time deciding, but I settled on gray.

When we got home, however, my decision didn't sit right. I began to think more and more about the shirt I *should've* gotten – the pink one with faint horizontal stripes. My dissatisfaction grew as I realized that my friend Colin wasn't worried about his t-shirt at all – he liked it just fine and probably hadn't thought about it for days.

A few days later, my fixations were still growing like kudzu, and Mom offered to drive me back to the restaurant so I could exchange my shirt. I had turned her down once or twice before, but things had gotten pretty tumultuous in my head, and I relented. *Fine,* I thought. *Let's just get this over with. Maybe then I'll be able to go down to the beach and enjoy things.*

When we got to the restaurant, though, my doubts multiplied. I could feel a tension building, a fizzy pressure in my head. I weighed the pros and cons of each shirt: the gray one was more traditionally cool, but the pink was bolder, full of a weird, preppy swagger. Gray wouldn't turn any heads, but maybe I didn't want heads turning – maybe I just wanted to get in under the radar. Pink was edgier, but it ran some real risks.

Mom tried to talk me through the decision, telling me to ask myself which one I liked better. She angled her head forward in determination, smacking her hands as if wiping them clean: "Just go with it."

I knew, at some level, that she was right, that thinking about things this way was tormenting me to no good end. But I couldn't decide. I didn't *know* which one was better. As soon as I leaned in one direction, I felt terrified that I might be missing out on everything the other shirt had to offer. After ten minutes of indecision, I burst into tears.

Mom stayed with me, but I suspect she was more unsettled than she let on. I'm not sure there had ever been an instance like this one, in which my ambivalence and indecision had risen to such acutely painful heights. I felt silly sitting there, aware of how privileged and prissy my concerns would look to most people. Here I was, a young boy on a nice beach vacation with his family, with a totally unnecessary T-shirt already in his possession, thrashing about because he thought there might be a slightly nicer one out there.

I was also aware of what I was missing. Everyone else was at the beach, playing or reading or crashing around in the surf. The beach itself was only a small road and a sand dune away. I didn't want to be here, but I didn't know how not to be.

It's fifth grade, I'm walking single-file down the hall with my classmates, and it occurs to me: my arms, swinging at my side, might graze the butt of the student in front of me. What then? What would that student think? What would he assume I was trying to do? Would he turn and face me down? Would he keep his thoughts to himself and later tell my classmates or the teacher? And what did it say about me that I was even thinking these things?

Then, a stranger and more nauseating turn: the images began to morph into what felt like memories – images so vivid and detailed that I couldn't tell the difference between a genuine recollection and an imposter. My mind divided into two voices, and each took its place behind the debating podium:

MATT BIEBER: Had I *already* touched the student in front of me? (If I had, wouldn't the denim of his pants feel just like what I'm imagining now – just like *this*?)

MATT BIEBER: But if I had touched him, wouldn't he have reacted – turned around, jumped away, snapped at me, *something*?

MATT BIEBER: Who knows? Different people probably respond to these things differently. If people think you're a pervert, they might not want to talk to you. They might think that if they ignore you, you'll just go away or try your sick impulses on someone else.

Or maybe he's scared, and he's doing his best to stay quiet and calm until he can get away from you and tell a teacher. Maybe you have a reputation as a kid who's obsessed with touching other children. Maybe everyone is just waiting to get home and tell their parents.

Or worst of all, maybe he already *did* respond. And maybe you immediately suppressed the memory of what happened and are now digging it back up. Maybe you have actually done what you're so afraid of doing, and maybe you really are exactly who you are so afraid of being. Are you capable of such perversion? And if you are, how do you know that this is the first time? Could there have been lots of other times just like this?

MATT BIEBER: Wait wait wait wait wait. What do you mean, 'How do you know that this is the first time?' First time for what? *You don't even know that anything happened.*

And that was true – I didn't know. But that wasn't particularly comforting; the stakes were too high. I ransacked my memory, looking for clues that would help me distinguish real memories from the junk shooting out of my geysery brain. But every time I tried to retrace my steps and arrange the events in sequence, the fog and spray reflected back into my eyes.

Over the course of the year, I found myself getting tied up in these thought-storms more and more. The wind in my brain would pick up, and I would quickly lose control of my thoughts. Ideas and feelings and images would sweep down my mind's thoroughfares, flipping cars and smashing storefront windows. After it had happened several times, I learned to see signs of the gathering clouds, but it didn't matter – I didn't know how to get out of the way.

Once, I found myself so full of torment that I did the only thing I could think to do. I got the attention of the student walking in front of me and asked, "Did I touch you by accident? I didn't mean to." And just as I began to speak, I detached from myself. From within my mental tornado, I watched this other Matt try to play it cool, to act normal, to pretend that this was the sort of thing that just happened, the sort of thing people brushed off.

But this other Matt didn't know what he was doing out there, all by himself. And he certainly had no idea how to take the other student's equivocal reaction. Was my classmate's mumbling and shrugging meant to tell me that it was no big deal, that I shouldn't worry? Was he just trying to tell me to leave him alone? Or was it something else entirely?

From within the whirlwind, I realized that my second self might not have said enough – that it might look like he was actually trying to paper things over and avoid the real issue. I found myself saying more: "I think I bumped you in the butt with my hand. I'm sorry."

Around this point, I felt a second split take place. I wasn't paying attention to the other student anymore – I wasn't even really talking to him. The words were plenty audible, but I was talking to myself. And the words weren't addressed to some problem that had taken place between me and my fellow student – they were slashing little efforts to penetrate the fog of fear in which I found myself.

Much more recently, I have come to understand that fear is the driving force behind obsessive-compulsive disorder. My therapist, Dr. M, has a perfect metaphor: OCD is like an overly active alarm system. It gets tripped all too often, and when it does, it fools the brain into believing that danger is lurking nearby. This triggers a wildly disproportionate fear response, which then reinforces the sense of danger. (If I weren't at risk, why would I be afraid?)

As a set of intellectual concepts, none of this is particularly complicated. What *is* complicated is understanding what's happening *while* it's happening and responding in a healthy way.

Perhaps complicated isn't quite the right word; maybe difficult is more appropriate. Either way, developing the capacity to see your mind's tumult in real-time takes a great deal of practice. Unfortunately, learning the basics of that practice was a good fifteen years in the future.

When I got my braces off at the beginning of ninth grade, my orthodontist sprang a trap: for the foreseeable future, I would now have to wear retainers day and night. Otherwise, my teeth might shift, undoing all the work of the previous three years and leaving me with a crooked, unsightly smile.

This was a bait-and-switch of the cruelest kind. Just as I was to be released onto the playing fields of high school, jaunty after rehab, I was hobbled with something worse – and far weirder – than braces: two discolored plastic retainers that made me lisp and spit. I had seen the finish line, and now I was being told that it was a mirage – and that I had months, even years, of feeling ugly and awkward ahead of me.

For the next several years, I oscillated. Sometimes I wore my retainers and felt resentful about it. Other times, I indignantly refused. But every time I failed to wear my retainers according to the orthodontist's schedule, I felt a creeping guilt that I suspected would one day bloom into something much bigger. It was the beginning of a pattern – a sense that things were perfect just as they were, but that I was on the verge of ruining them (or already in the process of doing so).

For the most part, though, my attention was directed elsewhere. At some point early in high school, I became fixated on the idea of going to a prestigious Ivy League school – Harvard or Princeton, or *maybe* Yale. I wanted to be around the smartest people I could find, and in an environment that would open up every possible door to success. I was sure that anything else would represent a failure to live up to my potential, and that I would spend my college years mired in frustration and disappointment.

In a certain way, I was repeating the pattern: I had been encouraged by my family and friends to think of myself as exceptionally talented, and I conceived of that talent as a kind of unblemished possibility, a perfect potential energy that would one day find expression in grand and noble ways. Until I found my calling, however, it was important to keep my options open, to keep climbing the ladder so that no one could deny me when my moment arrived. And for now, the only way to screw that up was by failing to achieve in school.

So I made sure I didn't. Throughout high school, I got near-perfect grades and monitored my class rank like a CIA analyst poring over threat reports from an unstable nuclear regime. (The regime's leader disguised herself as a kind, placid girl named Sarah. I sometimes found myself calculating the likelihood that she would overtake me in the race for valedictorian based on the number of weighted AP classes each of us was taking. She never did.)

I stacked up extracurriculars, too. I was on the wrestling, golf, tennis, and quiz bowl teams and president of a stupidly large number of school clubs. I got elected student representative to the district school board, then president of the student council. I founded a countywide chapter of Students for a Free Tibet.

Some of what I did genuinely interested me, but I also did everything with an eye to how it would play on my college applications. I knew I wasn't singularly brilliant at any one thing – I wasn't an Olympian or an inventor – so I had to be very good at lots of things.

All of this left relatively little time, however, for normal high school antics and experiences. I was just passing through, and I treated school like an instrument, a means to an end. And I suspected that that's how my classmates thought of me – a spectral, translucent presence, not someone who had any real investment in this place or these people. Luckily, I was often still included socially. But that inclusion felt thin, and I chalked it up to my close friends' popularity. I didn't know people very well; I didn't have much to say to them, nor they to me.

During my senior year, I made the varsity wrestling team. It had been five years since I last made the varsity as a branchy 12-year-old on the middle school squad. That year, I had competed in the 80 lb. weight class. It was my first experience cutting weight, and I was hyper-scrupulous, refusing to eat anything more than my anxiety-driven standards would permit. Better to clear the bar by a good margin, my thinking went, than to eat a bit more dinner and then spend all day fretting over my crimes. Sometimes, I would weigh in as many as three pounds under the limit. I suspect that seventh grade was the year Mom's hair began to gray.

I was never a particularly good wrestler, and after middle school, I wandered in the junior varsity wilderness, becoming accustomed to its unsupervised and indifferent terrain. For the most part, this was fine with me. I was juggling a million other commitments, arranging my battalions for an assault on the Ivy League, so it was nice to be able to skip practice now and again. No one relied on me, and there was a kind of casual sleepiness about the whole affair. JV wrestlers didn't have to worry about our weight, for example – close enough was good enough, and no one conducted weigh-ins before matches. The matches themselves were held just prior to the varsity contests, and they unfolded on no certain schedule – as if the coaches and referees were stretching in advance of the main event. A few dedicated parents polka-dotted the stands, the cheerleaders straggled in, and the varsity squad hung back in the locker room, waiting.

I wondered what it felt like to be in that locker room. I imagined solitary warriors in quiet, somber preparation, finding their ways into mental spaces that mirrored the moment's import.

When a varsity opening at 145 lbs. appeared during my senior year, I leapt at the chance. The wrestlers at 138 and 152 were district and state qualifiers, way out of my league. At 145, however, it was just one younger, less experienced kid and I. If I could cut seven pounds and fend him off, I would be able to enter the company of men.

In some ways, making the team was exactly what I'd hoped for. All of a sudden, I was taken seriously by guys who – in my eyes, at least – had crossed an intangible but definitive frontier into manhood. They were strong and talented, many of them chiseled through a physical discipline that I couldn't fathom. They were also experienced; many of them drank, some of them smoked pot, and a few were having sex with impossibly hot girls. Most importantly, though, they had borne weight on their shoulders – the weight of wrestling under the lights, in front of the crowds, on behalf of the team.

It was to this last category that I was admitted. There was a new affection from the varsity guys, a brotherliness. Some of that was just pragmatic, of course. After all, how I performed affected them now. But it was more than that as well. There was a respect, a quiet understanding that we were part of something important.

Of course, being a part of the team meant showing devotion in strange ways. Cutting weight was the least of it, and that alone could be pretty bizarre. There were the standard tricks – wearing plastic trash bags and a couple of sets of sweats to practice, putting a bag of ice on the thermostat. There was the yo-yoing around matches – salads and Freeze Pops the night before, McDonald's afterward. (I once saw my friend Ben weigh in 10 pounds over the limit on the morning of a match. I don't know how he made weight by 4:15 that afternoon, but I can guess.) There were some reliable desperation moves, like spitting in a cup throughout the bus ride to an away match.

On two separate occasions, I jerked off in order to cut a few final ounces. One of those times was in a public restroom at an opposing team's high school; when we arrived, I leapt off the bus, peeled away from the team, and found a relatively hidden restroom stall. When other people entered the restroom, I ratcheted back activities, doing my best to think hot thoughts and perform quiet maintenance work. After several maddening stop-and-start episodes, I managed a surprisingly pleasurable finish, (given the circumstances) quickly calculated the likely weight of the tissues in my hand, reassembled my clothes, and sprinted to the locker rooms for weigh-ins. I stripped down, wondering if my coaches would detect the smell, and made weight by a hair.

I suspect that almost everyone on the team had at least one similarly outlandish tale. In general, though, that kind of behavior was rare. More absurd were the ways that cutting weight rewired our everyday brains. I thought about the weight of piss and spit and haircuts, and I became acutely conscious of my own fecal output. Because I wasn't eating much, production was grudging. I silently placated the intestinal gods for bounteous harvests, and I rejoiced when they occasionally arrived. I also conducted visual inspections for size and density, doing my best to translate these qualities into pounds and ounces. (To this day, I find myself silently noting the total volume of shit in the bowl as I pull my pants up and reach for the flush.)

Does it need to be said? High school wrestlers often have distorted and nonsensical relationships with their bodies (much like people who worry about their weight for other reasons). Sometimes, our proximity to bodily weirdness led to behavior that had nothing to do with making weight. This included a general indifference to minor maladies. One guy's girlfriend showed up at school looking like Gorbachev, a continent of impetigo across her forehead. I watched another kid leave a two-hour practice soaked in sweat, ringworm tracks all down his leg, without so much as a shower. I wasn't any better. Once I got cauliflower ear and walked around with pus-filled lobes for a month before the pain forced me to the doctors.

In December of my senior year, I got accepted to Princeton. It wasn't quite the culminating, celebratory occasion it might have been. Instead, it was a moment mixed with relief and regret. On the one hand, I could finally take my foot off the accelerator – nothing I did or failed to do in school would matter as much anymore. On the other hand, this was a victory in a battle I hadn't really wanted to fight. I had wanted to go to Harvard, but I'd suspected that I had a better chance to get into Princeton. (Applicants were only permitted to apply early to one Ivy League school, when admission chances were highest.) And because the thought of not getting into either school was unbearable, I had played the numbers and done the 'safe' thing.

I realize it's probably hard to be sympathetic with these concerns, and I'm not asking for sympathy. I know that going to either school – that going to college at all – was a blessing. But I didn't have that kind of perspective then. My brain was wired to worry, and for three years, I had had one very big thing to worry about. When my admission letter arrived, that worry dissipated. And as it did, an older and more insidious one re-appeared.

A few months later, I was returning to wrestling practice from a bathroom break when I caught sight of myself in a mirror. I must have smiled or made a face, because I noticed something that stopped me short: my top front teeth looked crooked. I moved closer. I was right – my teeth didn't make a flat wall anymore. Instead, one of my front teeth stuck out a bit further than the other. Light caught on the protruding ridge, casting the recessed tooth into a slight shadow.

I headed back to practice and tried to dismiss what I had seen. And amazingly, given what was to come, I managed to do so fairly well.

Later that spring, during a tennis match with my friend Dan, I felt my tongue slip across a ridge on the back of my upper teeth that I'd never felt before. For a moment, I felt objective and detached about the situation. I was a journalist with double confirmation: there was some truth to this story. But detachment quickly gave way.

Over the coming weeks, I began to pay more and more attention to my teeth – feeling around them with my tongue, trying to convince myself that that ridge had been there all along, that I simply hadn't noticed. One day, I stood in front of the bathroom mirror, hoping to settle things once and for all. The truth of the matter was a high, cold wall: my left front tooth rose up over my right, like one tectonic plate submerging another.

I was distraught. This was exactly what I had worried about for so long, but I had never imagined that the guilt and regret would be nearly this intense. I had had a perfectly attractive smile, and now it was gone. I had put in years of hard, embarrassing work with braces and retainers, and now I had nothing to show for them. I might as well have never had braces in the first place.

I've never been more conscious of time's incontrovertible forward motion. I wanted to roll it back, but I could feel myself bumping up against an almost palpable barrier. *This is how things are. Your life is like this now.*

Unless – unless I could repair the damage. I stuck my hands in my mouth and attempted to wrench my teeth back into place, pressing the left tooth backward and torqueing the right tooth forward until a bizarre pressure came from what felt like the insides of the teeth themselves. I removed my hands and inspected my mouth once again. My teeth didn't look any better. And wait: were they now even more out of place?

I couldn't quite tell, but the more I thought about it, the more likely it seemed. After all, what good could possibly come from trying to wrench my teeth around? There's a reason that orthodontists take years to fix crooked teeth – because our bodies aren't meant to be messed with in this way.

The guilt crashed through my levees, sweeping aside trees and homes. How could I have been so stupid and irresponsible, so wishful and naïve? This was an entirely new level of pain, a head rush of almost sonic intensity. I would have given anything to go back to the hell of five minutes before.

The pattern was now established: Step one: notice something that seems awry. Step two: construct a narrative in which a once-perfect situation has degraded through my irresponsibility. Step three: try to intervene, only to make the situation worse. Step four: feel overcome with desperate guilt and shame.

Over the coming years, this pattern would become much more elaborate, full of tendrils and filaments. It would also crop up in nearly every area of my life – coloring my relationships, toying with my ambitions and desires, and colonizing past, present, and future. For now, though, my OCD was apparently satisfied with a head full of worries about a mouthful of crooked teeth.

As the school year wound down, life dismantled itself. I made close friends with mirrors, inspecting my teeth at every opportunity. I had favorite reflective surfaces, both at home and elsewhere. These were the ones that provided the most charitable views of my teeth – whose light and angles could be made to flatter, so long as I cocked my head just so. I would spend minutes on end in front of the glass, yawning my jaw and examining my upper teeth from every possible vantage point. Over and over I would search the same territory, eyes hungry for flaws, stomach terrified that I would find them.

I did most of this spelunking on my own, living for the little niches in the day when no one was around. Sometimes, though, the urge to inspect reared its head in company. In those cases, I did my best to be surreptitious, flashing my teeth at mirrors when backs were turned. And when I couldn't be stealthy, I made up excuses for my behavior: *Did I have food in my teeth? Just gonna check real quick. Huh! Nothing there. It sure feels like it – how strange! Better check again.*

Mere visual observation wasn't always enough. I expanded my toolkit, inserting fingers and feeling around for signs of movement or evidence of instability. Of course, there was always a Heisenberg risk: as I sought to observe, I might well move my teeth around even more. But the analysis simply had to go forward. Amid the emotional firestorm, I did my scientifically rigorous best. And while I dutifully recorded the results, I felt the lab burning around me.

While parts of me were closing down, others were opening. K had been a friend, but never just. When my prom date canceled, I asked K. We attended with another couple, but K and I couldn't see or hear them, our eyes and our thoughts searching out one another's. We danced and goofed around, and at one point she chased me outside. I let her catch me, and we collided and slid down a small swale. We lay in a heap, stunned, looking for our bearings and knowing they were very nearby. When I dropped her off at the end of the night, K told me she thought she was falling in love.

As the summer wound down, it became more and more difficult to hide my suffering from my parents. One day, as we sat and talked about what college might be like, I let a little water through the dam, hinting at my teeth-related worries. All of a sudden, I found myself talking and talking. I told them about the scenarios I envisioned – about the hordes of beautiful, young, prep-schooled Aryans who would take one look at my wretched smile and judge me an ugly peasant. About the professors who would see my teeth as stigmata, evidence of profound unworthiness. In the elite world of Princeton, I imagined that perfect teeth were a shibboleth. And because I didn't have them, I would be excluded from all of the intellectual, social, and sexual experiences that I most wanted. I had ruined college before it even began, and I had done so from the depths of my own degraded character.

As I choked out half-sentences, tears crashing down my cheeks, I felt another kind of shame. I was going to Princeton, for God's sake, and I didn't know how to appreciate my own good fortune. Across the room, my dad sat quietly, looking at me with an expression I found hard to read. I imagined all kinds of disgusted thoughts running through his head. After all, he'd grown up without much money. He'd been first person in his family to go to college, and he'd done it alone, chinning his way up as best he could. I, on the other hand, couldn't have had it easier. How could I be such a fucking softie?

Mom sat next to me on the couch, tender and patient and rooted to her seat with concern. She looked me square in the eyes, trying her best to understand what was going on inside. She knew she couldn't quite see it, couldn't grasp what had such a grip on me. She suggested a visit to the dentist to see if we could get my teeth fixed. She also suggested we make an appointment for me to "see someone."

Mom ended up reaching out to Dr. K, the same woman I'd seen a few times as a little boy when Mom and Dale were getting divorced. It was strange going back to her office. I had driven by it thousands of times since those visits a dozen years before, but I'm not sure I could have even pointed it out.

Dr. K's office was in her home, and going in, that seemed too casual. As she guided me up the stairs to her office, I felt the presence of the rest of the house, all that mundane domestic stuff undermining what we were about to do. I wanted more distance between the kitchen where she cooked SpaghettiOs for her kids and the office where she would try to rescue me from hell.

These feelings didn't last. I took a seat in a soft chair and she was kind to me, and in a few minutes, I was falling through space, that silhouette in the opening credits of *Mad Men*. My head felt lighter, looser, as if the tension that I'd been storing there was burning off. I couldn't tell whether any of this was good or bad, but it did feel like I was seeing a little more clearly. I wasn't just a spoiled, weak-willed boy with no self-control. I wasn't just infected with bad ideas, and I wasn't just incompetent because I couldn't think my way past them. There was something real here, something true and wildly awry. And as I glimpsed its edges, a frightening new thought bubbled up: what if this wasn't the kind of thing that I could overcome?

None of what was happening seemed to surprise Dr. K, though, and that was a comfort. She had seen this before. This was something that could be seen. Maybe it was even something we could name and respond to. We talked for a little while longer, and then Dr. K led me into an adjoining room and left me to complete a test with several hundred multiple-choice questions. The questions seemed designed to get at my basic mental patterns – When did I worry, how long did the worries last, and how much anxiety did they cause? How might I respond to such-and-such a situation? Did I believe this or that?

Like a polygraph, many of the questions were repeated with slightly different variations – perhaps to try to catch out the truth, to make sure that I didn't just answer in the ways that I thought would sound best. This struck me as funny. I'd already done the hard part, I thought – unfurling my private embarrassments in front of a stranger. It seemed silly to undermine myself after overcoming a hurdle like that.

That day, Dr. K hinted at what she thought was going on, but I don't think I received her final diagnosis until a few weeks later. I had OCD. And unfortunately, I wouldn't do anything about it for another two years.

In the meantime, college was barreling closer, and I couldn't stop thinking about my teeth. We went to see my dentist, and he performed a cosmetic procedure, adding a small layer of material to my recessed front tooth to bring it in line with the others. (He also suggested a whitening treatment, confirming my anxieties about my teeth's yellowish tinge. I agreed.)

After the procedure, I went to the restroom to inspect. All things being equal, I suppose my teeth looked a bit better. But my smile also looked enormously strange to me, like it had been made for a slightly different face. What were these swoops and angles? I couldn't tell – was I newly beautiful and simply unable to appreciate my movie-star smile? Or was I monstrous, my every grin revealing a dental toupee, a freakish badge of overpowering insecurity?

The dentist, his staff, and Mom all assured me that things looked great, and thankfully, I was more or less able to believe them. I was embarrassed as hell about what I had done – particularly around my dad – but most people didn't know. All they saw was a pretty smile, and that seemed alright.

Except, inevitably, it didn't stay alright. My teeth looked nice *now*, sure. But they would continue to shift, and then I would be right back where I started. (I had asked the dentist about inserting a permanent brace behind my teeth to hold them in place. He had told me that I would need to see an orthodontist for that, but I couldn't bear the prospect of returning to that world.)

So I quickly resumed my habits – gazing into the mirror, running my tongue over my teeth, feeling about with my fingers like a scholar studying runes. When I talked, I often knew exactly where my upper, lower teeth, and tongue were in relation to one another, and how much pressure my tongue was exerting on my most vulnerable teeth. When I ate, I placed my food in my mouth delicately and chewed deliberately, keen to avoid any unnecessary clacking. When I kissed my girlfriend, I modulated the way our lips collided, making sure I was leading equally with left and right sides and pulling up into lighter kisses to give my teeth a break every so often. Risk was everywhere, and if I was going to slow the pace of my smile's decay, I had to be vigilant. I became ever more observant, noticing subtler and subtler risks to my teeth's positioning and developing elaborately detailed beliefs about my oral anatomy.

For the most part, I kept these ideas to myself. I knew no one would take them seriously, and I didn't want to hear about how I was being silly, how the world didn't really work this way. Had anyone else thought about their teeth the way I had? Had anyone else really considered the risks we took with them every day? No – they just blithely ate their spareribs and fell face-first into pillows, twirling and dancing on the edges of cliffs.

CHAPTER TWO

"Ugh, ow," I thought, "will I get to like this? And if I don't,
how do I get to leave?

-JACK KEROUAC, *THE DHARMA BUMS*

A t the beach when we were young, Colin and Adrian and I would
play a game called Deadman. We'd lay facedown in the surf where
the waves crashed onto the shore, letting the water take us wherever
it would. Coming up for air occasionally was okay, but it was far better
to go limp, to surrender, to allow yourself to be flipped and twisted and
served up onto the sand.

During my freshman year of college, I forgot how to surrender
entirely. Instead, I fought a never-ending struggle with wave after wave
of obsessions and compulsions.

I arrived at Princeton early for a university-organized camping trip.
We would spend the first night on campus before boarding a bus and
heading to the forests.

That night, my group spread our tarps and sleeping bags in the
grass just outside the university's gates. The late summer air was still

pleasantly warm, the clear sky above speckled with occasional stars. Alongside us, the blue and gray Gothic stone walls patiently supported slate roofs.

For just a moment, I felt cocooned. This place was no longer an aspiration – it was ours. We could sleep outside these walls, confident that we were welcome within them. We could go away camping, knowing that these rooms would be waiting for us when we returned. I registered the buzz among my fellow students, excitement rocketing around inside us. Most of us had probably worked very hard for this moment; now, I suspected, each of us was absorbing its truth in his or her own way.

I tried to soak it all in, but it was difficult – my teeth kept blocking the way. Soon after we laid out our pillows and sleeping bags, I excused myself and jogged up to a second-floor bathroom for a tooth inspection. Luckily, not many students had arrived yet, so I had the bathroom largely to myself. It was surreal, importing my routines from home into these towers that I had dreamt about so much. This wasn't what I was here for.

I went back downstairs and tried to rejoin the conversation, but every half-hour or so, my worries would get the better of me. When I plopped down onto my pillow, had I undone my smile? When I made a hard 'g' sound, had everything changed? As the students around me went to sleep, irony and disappointment squabbled bitterly in my mind. I had sacrificed so much to be here, and I wanted to play the astronaut strutting across the gangplank with his team, about to board the vessel but reveling in the moment just before. But my worries didn't care about my schedule; launch would be delayed.

I was assigned to an eight-man suite, and we paired off into tiny rooms with bunk beds and lockless doors. All of a sudden, I was surrounded by bodies, and I no longer had the private space that I had come to rely on. If I was going to continue to monitor my teeth, I would have to change my tactics.

So after lunch each day, when few of my roommates were around, I would return to my room for a thorough tooth examination. Were things where I expected them to be? Or had the situation deteriorated? On occasion, I would feel pleasantly surprised by a first impression - *Look at that charming smile, those well-aligned teeth!* But as soon as I turned the kaleidoscope, looking for confirmation from different angles and under different light, my confidence would disintegrate. It was like watching a theater crew deconstruct a set – for just a moment, I had been buoyed by the illusions on stage. Quickly, however, the truth of the matter, the whole Potemkin disappointment, was revealed. I would stand transfixed, captivated by the rotting, crooked, yellowing floorboards, sensing the abyss beneath.

It wasn't all ineffable pain. There were words, too, a ticker-tape narration: *Girls won't want you, your teachers won't like you, and you don't belong here. Your whole presence here is a sham, and the only way you can keep it up is by running at speeds that you'll never maintain. You're a masturbating, nose-picking, shit-smelling disaster, an ugly, entropic little pinball playing a game you can't possibly win. You don't deserve sympathy, and no one feels any.*

You can see how things would balloon. I would start by fixating on my teeth, but soon the worries would expand, an angry universe unfurling outward. My teeth weren't just teeth; they were a proxy for the rest of me, a referendum on my entire disgraceful character.

During most of these sessions, nothing existed outside that bathroom. I might have been Charlie in the Great Glass Elevator, an astronaut floating through space in a dingy, yellow-lit box. Thoughts came in panicky pulses. Time slowed. My entire being – past, present, and future – lived in the space between me and the mirror. And my reflection was a pissed-off oracle, dispensing predictions that sounded much more like sentences.

But if the future seemed desolate, I wasn't entirely without options. I was a man. I had a mind for imagining things and hands to make them real. Reshaping my teeth with my fingers was off the table, but what about other tools?

I began to brush my teeth strategically, applying heavy pressure on the right tooth from behind and assaulting the left tooth from the front. Sometimes, I would pause mid-brush to see whether my efforts were taking effect. (This always felt like cheating, though, the weak faith of the cowardly.) Other times, I would simply brush, spit, and walk away, hoping that my petitions would be answered.

At one level, I wasn't fooling myself. I was a cheap lawyer who'd found a loophole in my own legal code; brushing my teeth this way was no different in spirit than trying to renovate my smile with my fingers. On the other hand, I had to brush, and there was no way to tell what effects mindless brushing might have. What if my default brushing patterns actually compounded the damage by applying disproportionate pressure in the wrong places? Things were already out of joint, and becoming more so all the time. Even if I brushed my teeth with perfectly balanced pressure, wasn't that likely to make things worse?

So I made my compromise. I wasn't going to intervene directly, but if it just so happened that my teeth shifted back where I wanted them because of my tactical toothbrushing, well, what could be the harm in that?

In some ways, I had founded my own little religion. I'm not sure there was any object of worship, exactly, and I didn't really think anyone was going to answer my prayers. But I certainly had established a great many rituals, and I lived by them.

"Ritual" is a curious word. Psychologists use the term to describe the behaviors that OCD sufferers take up in order to relieve the pressure caused by their intrusive thoughts. *Please – anything to make this feeling go away. Take another look in the mirror? Of course! Feel around with my tongue just to make sure that nothing moved during lunch? No problem!*

For me, these rituals began as ad hoc ways of propitiating vengeful deities. Pretty soon, though, they became ingrained patterns, rules that couldn't be broken. *What do we do after lunchtime? We go back to the room and check our teeth. And what happens if we don't? Let's not think about that – that shit show is the whole reason we created these rules in the first place.*

All of a sudden, these stopgap solutions had started to look more like wisdom. No, it wasn't pleasant to make my daily pilgrimage to the bathroom. And yes, it was shockingly painful to open my mouth for inspection under those harsh lights. But these were the things I did – these were the things I *had* to do – if I was to maintain some kind of order.

But describing it like this – as an effort to maintain order – might give you the wrong idea. I wasn't assessing my options, evaluating the pros and cons of each potential course of action. These weren't *choices* that I was making – not on the first day, and not on any of the days thereafter.

Does a kettle choose to let off steam? These were simply things that happened. I would eat, I would flood with fear, and I would find myself walking to the bathroom. I would open my mouth, I would flood with fear, and I would see myself leaning in for a better look.

My rituals were a way to cope. The trouble, of course, is that they didn't work like they were supposed to. And how could they? OCD is a tripwire calibrated to the faintest touch. When the alarms went off, my tendency was to check and see what had gone wrong, to inspect the premises for intruders. But of course, this inspection was never objective or scientific. Instead, it was conducted under conditions of panic.

And that may be the most fundamental thing to understand: OCD is a kind of self-imposed emotional extortion. The trouble is, extortion doesn't happen on your terms – you don't pay protection money to the mafia just once. First, you pay a one-time fee. Then it's a regular, monthly transaction. And soon enough, you pay whenever the hell the mob shows up.

I also took classes. Princeton had its share of famous professors, and I thought I was lucky to have classes with several of them during my first semester. I attended an ethics seminar with the philosopher Peter Singer, and my introductory economics course was taught by *New York Times* columnist (and later Nobel laureate) Paul Krugman. Other prominent intellectuals and social theorists circulated too, electrons in a cloud of intellectual ferment.

Before arriving on campus, I had looked upon some of these figures as oracles – beings that would furnish me with life's secrets if I managed to find my way into their company. The first semester, then, provided some important disillusionment. Peter Singer may have been a powerful thinker – his book *Animal Liberation* had led me to convert to veganism a few weeks before arriving to school – but he was also very clearly human, with an endearing awkwardness about him. When he spoke behind a podium, he rocked from side to side, the tic of a nervous middle-schooler presenting before an untrustworthy class.

Krugman's economic analyses may have earned him the respect of his colleagues, and his rhetorical skills may have earned him a column in a prestigious newspaper, but as a professor, he wasn't much to speak of. His lectures were both doctrinal – dry recountings of conventional economic premises – and full of academic inside baseball that meant nothing to a first-time student like me.

Sometimes, Professor Krugman wasn't even there. At the time, Argentina was in the midst of an economic crisis, and Krugman missed several classes in order to fly down and provide assistance. I didn't begrudge him his absence, exactly, but I was beginning to get the sense that the teacher-student relationship in college wasn't going to be exactly what I had imagined. As students, we often weren't our professors' first concern. In many cases, they had been teaching their courses for many years; when the semester rolled around, some instructors seemed to do little more than pull their lecture notes out of a drawer.

Even the basic concept of a lecture – that staple of college curricula that had once seemed so romantic – began to feel strange. We students would walk through Gothic arches, climb creaky wooden steps, and find seats in beautiful rooms, just as the brochures and websites had advertised. But then – and it became harder and harder to look past this reality – we would listen as a professor would read off a piece of paper for fifty minutes. Sometimes, there was time for questions, but in other cases, professors simply delivered uninterrupted monologues. I found myself wondering: why all the pomp and circumstance, all the anxiety and competition and prestige, for information I could have spent ten minutes reading in my own room?

I had always read a great deal, but in college, my habit acquired new dimensions. Here I was, with the opportunity to read and learn alongside brilliant and original thinkers. I felt responsible for vacuuming up every page of every book or article that I'd been assigned, and that anything less would represent a failure of character. Over the next several years, this habit would metastasize to the point where it was no longer about assignments. Reading was its own end, and everything else – socializing, relaxation, whatever – had to be sacrificed at its altar.

When I moved to New York after college, my reading attained comically absurd proportions. I was working a job that didn't mean anything to me, so I leaned on reading to provide my missing sustenance. I read in the three minutes before the subway train arrived, then during the two bumpy stops before I arrived at my destination, doing my best to not slosh too aggressively into my neighbors. I read during the one-to-four-minute period between signing in at the dentist's office and answering the assistant's chirrupy call (which, really, was barely enough time to get situated in a chair, deposit my bags and coats and umbrellas around me in a half-gesture of respect for other patients' space, find my bookmark, and begin). Elevator rides, sometimes. The wait at my halal chicken lunch spot.

Even in college, though, I was already reading huntedly, chased and chasing. I read constantly, in all the gaps of my day. I read to lose myself, to escape from the din in my own head and into the inferno of others'. (For this reason, I've never cared much about plot, and I've tended to feel bizarrely repelled by genre fiction. All I really want is to spend some time in the heads of characters that feel like plausible human beings, who aren't irretrievable, villainous, one-note monsters. Which might be the same thing.)

As long as I continued reading, I found it difficult to stop, no matter how terrible a book's prose. But looking up, responding to my name, answering the phone – these could break the spell and help me get my distance. The trouble was, too much distance meant disorientation. What was I when I wasn't reading? So I read to locate myself, too.

For all my devotion to books, I was surprisingly disloyal to specific books. When I found myself disengaged – either because I was unimpressed or actually repulsed by what I was reading – I felt a deep stress. Should I continue? Why? Why, when there are other glorious books out there, books that didn't make me feel this way? But then, of course, the problem became distinguishing the rough patches in a truly good book from the rough patches which indicate that a book isn't very good. (And did it matter which was which? There were probably books out there without rough patches, so why not just read those?)

There was also my respect for books more broadly, which had a way of bathing even the most useless volumes in its rays. And there was my compulsive attachment to achievement – to the idea that finishing would count for something. As if other people were paying attention, and they'd notice that I was now the type of person who'd read *Mrs. Dalloway* or *The Brothers Karamazov*. Sometimes, I would doubt that these accomplishments really accumulated in any meaningful way, or whether it even made sense to think of them as accomplishments. In these moments, reading was a conveyor belt running backward from zero – I had to keep at it, but the most I could hope to do was stay even.

Other times, though, I would imagine a better self beckoning me from beyond the final page. That self was wiser, more edified, more refined, more in control. *Just a bit more*, it whispered. *You don't want to stop now – a life-changing insight might be a couple of pages away. What a tragedy it would be to miss out when you're this close.* Then, as I approached the end of a book, I'd realize that finishing wasn't going to change anything; I was still going to be the same person – a straining, gasping little soul seeking instructions on how to live.

Every now and again, though, I encountered a book that seemed to promise the guidance I so badly wanted. The flashes at the end of Baldwin's *Go Tell it on the Mountain*; the thunderbolts throughout Dostoevsky; Virginia Woolf's conviction that paying attention might provide enough grist to make a life. But then what? The moment would pass, and I'd continue skimming along the pages, half convinced that living in books was the only kind of salvation available. Nothing had any staying power. Books changed everything for an hour or two, and then you went back to living the same stumbling life as before.

Throughout my freshman year, a bowling-ball battery of teeth-related worries kept my pins tottering on their edges. Sometimes, I found myself hoping they would fall, if only to relieve the tension. (Once, I told K that I had pictured smashing my own teeth with a hammer. She moaned a soft "No" and hugged me tightly.)

Meanwhile, a second ball was hurtling down the lane. When it struck, the few pins left standing would explode outward, colliding against one another in a crazy-making thunderclap.

Every few weeks, K and I would trade visits – I would drive down to her school in suburban Philadelphia, or she would take the SEPTA/Amtrak train combination out to New Jersey. During one of these weekends, K and I were wandering around Princeton, looping and musing through the streets. Something in a basement-level shop window caught my attention, and I leaned over, placing my hands on my thighs and gripping the denim of my jeans between my fingers. As I did so, I felt – or thought I felt – a quick rub in my crotch. A worry arose: *Am I pressing my testicles together?* I frantically examined my consciousness: one search party flashed its lights across my memories from a split-second before, while another sought to pin down exactly what was taking place in the moment. (Even now I'm not sure of the sequence of things. Did the feeling arise first, the initial domino in a chain of subsequent thoughts? Or was there no physical feeling? Did the entire thing happen in my mind?)

I suspected that this was one of those times when my brain was leaping the tracks, and I didn't want to be too reactive. I held my position, bent toward the shop window but insensible to anything outside my mind. Images and possibilities flashed across my field of vision, constellations of denim and soft tissue. I saw my testicles colliding and merging, a Venn diagram of beige and pink. *No please no not this. Don't take this away too. Not sex. Not now. Not at the beginning.*

Sex with K had been a first for both of us. Outside of kissing, just about everything had been. We'd experimented throughout the summer, and a couple of months later, she had decided that she was ready. (Not surprisingly, I had been ready for a while, and it hadn't felt like any decisions were involved.) The first couple of times we tried, though, it didn't work.

I hadn't realized this was a possibility – I knew you could be bad at sex, but I didn't think you could fail at the basic mechanics. But for whatever reason, we couldn't make it happen. There was something in her, blocking the way; I still don't know whether it was an unbroken hymen or just a kind of tension, an uncertainty.

Strangely, it wasn't a big deal. We laughed about it and looked at medical photos on the Internet, wondering if this was the sort of thing that happened to other couples. K consulted her mom, a physician's assistant. We tried for a couple of weekends, and then – with no warning or reasoning – something changed.

EPILOGUE

Of course, OCD infiltrated my budding sex life, just as it had set up shop in every other arena of my existence. I could write about all of that, and perhaps someday I will. But for now, I have to bring this narrative to an inconclusive end.

Toward the beginning of this work, I described the suspicion that had discouraged me from writing about OCD. I didn't want this to be about trying to redeem myself, about trading my experiences for the illusory security that might come with publishing a book. From a Buddhist perspective, I didn't want this to be about ego.

A word of clarification about that term – ego – might be useful. From a Buddhist perspective, ego is understood as a basic – but profound – mistake, one that undergirds everything else about how we experience the world. In the words of the contemporary Tibetan teacher Chögyam Trungpa: "Confused mind is inclined to view itself as a solid, ongoing thing, but it is only a collection of tendencies, events." In other words, when we talk about our "selves," we imagine that there is something there – a "self," whatever that might be.

If this were just a casual inclination, one habit among many, perhaps it wouldn't be such a big deal. But as Trungpa teaches – and as my own experience bears out – confused mind isn't just *inclined* to view itself as a real entity. Rather, it holds tenaciously to this view, using an enormous variety of psychological and interpersonal tricks. And it does so because it imagines that a great deal is at stake. As Trungpa would say, fundamentally, we're afraid that we don't exist. And most of the time, our minds are whirling at a thousand miles an hour in order to keep ourselves busy and occupied – anything, so long as we don't have to glimpse the possibility that we aren't real in the ways we imagine.

This work has become exactly that – an effort to prove to myself that I am real, a solid thing capable of producing other solid (and in this case, book-shaped) things. It is about trying to gain ground, to have a way to account for and defend my existence. And for that reason, continuing with the project has begun to feel aggressive and claustrophobic.

Now, that isn't *all* that's going on. To be sure, I've had a number of richly rewarding and illuminating writing sessions, moments in which I saw aspects of my life with new clarity and compassion. But between each of those sessions, my mind tends to fixate on the baseball card stats: How many pages have I written? How many chapters? Have I written enough – and in the right ways – to put together a book proposal? What if I just serialized what I've written so far, published it on my blog, and tried to catch a publisher's eye?

In other words, there are at least two sets of motivations in play, and I spend far more time immersed in the unpalatable ones than writing from the nobler ones.

My ego-oriented fixations have also begun to infect the way I approach the writing itself; I spend as much time worrying about whether my sentences are elegant enough as I do looking into myself and trying to see what's going on. For this reason, I find myself avoiding the writing. And even when I do find my way back into those less ambitious and more exploratory states of mind, all of that is quickly swamped as soon as I hit "save" and walk away.

Ego is winning, and the more I look at my experience, the more it has begun to feel as if that outcome was baked into the nature of the project. After all, I was never writing purely out of inspiration and passion. I was also seeking to meet a particular set of institutional requirements – a page count, a set of stylistic considerations, and a range of concepts about what constituted legitimate or worthwhile work. In other words, I was seeking to produce a *thing*, just as my ego was seeking to use the project to reinforce itself.

During Buddhism's early centuries, monks (known as *bhikkus*) developed the *Patimokkha* – a code of discipline for monastic communities. This code regulated all kinds of things: how to eat, speak, avoid illegitimate sexual encounters, and so on. When I read the code recently, however, what struck me most deeply were the rules around possessions – in particular, the length of time *bhikkus* were allowed to keep gifts. A *bhikku* could accept certain small gifts – a bowl, say, or a bolt of cloth – if he could actually foresee a need for the item in the near term. Stockpiling possessions for some indeterminate future, however, cut against *bhikku* discipline.

These passages called to mind my own relationship to personal property. As a young boy, I collected sports cards. Like many of my friends, I amassed thousands of cards, rigorously organizing them and keeping close watch on their fluctuating values.

More recently, though, the impulse toward collecting – and even toward just preserving what I have – has reversed. Over the last couple of years, I've taken enormous relief in getting rid of what I own – carting boxes of books to the library, ruthlessly plundering my closet for clothes to give to Goodwill, and deleting a music collection comprising thousands of songs. The pleasure even extends to more transient possessions – sifting through the mail and tossing the junk.

Possessions have begun to feel like weight, like wildly overpriced insurance policies against the future. The fewer of them I have, the lighter I feel, and the more capable I become of living in a present that makes no promises.

If I'm going to continue to write, I suspect it will have to be in that same spirit – not in order to seek validation or collect something for myself, but as a means of clarifying something I'm seeing and then giving it away. While I was home sick recently, I found myself motivated to write in just this way. Some things came to mind, I explored them for a little while, and when ego-oriented anxieties began to clog my mind, I posted the piece on my blog and walked away. Here is what I wrote:

I haven't left the house much over the last couple of days. My sheets are bunched up at the foot of the bed, clothes are strewn all over the floor, and containers of half-eaten soup and Emergen-C survey the wasteland from their perches on desktops and chairs.

It's a lot like a silent meditation retreat – just sitting and watching my thoughts and emotions arise and then fade away. Of course, I'm spending my time this way for different reasons. In an electricity-less retreat cabin in the woods, it's because there's little else to do, and because that's what you're there for. Here at home, it's because I don't have the energy to do anything else.

And that's a blessing. Because as I watch my mind churn out thoughts, I'm seeing just how much time I spend trying to get away from myself. I want to be distracted, occupied, *busy*. I want some activity that will make me feel like I'm doing something 'productive' with my time – and it almost doesn't matter what it is. Watch reruns of *Parks* and *Recreation* again? Sure! Organize the spice rack? Why not! What I want, I think, is to feel that I'm passing time in a way that other people would recognize, that would count as an answer to the question "What did you do today?"

But over these last few days, I haven't had the energy to do those sorts of things. And as I've considered them, I've often felt repelled by the sheer transparency of my strategies, of my desire to do anything but spend time alone. In Buddhist terms, I've felt revulsion at the way my mind is constantly grasping after something – something solid, something pleasurable, something other than *this*.

And even in those very moments of insight, the grasping instinct reasserts itself. Too tired to get up and make dinner? Why not just stay here and check e-mail on your phone? Or tick off those little tasks you've accrued in your 'Notes' app? This instinct can begin to sound like wisdom: *You're not dead, are you? So you ought to be able to get* something *done.*

But if I listen closely, I realize that this isn't the voice of wisdom – it's the voice of neurosis, of an ego that doesn't know how to be in the world without creating a never-ending stream of tasks to accomplish. When I translate, this is how it sounds: do stuff do stuff do stuff do stuff do stuff.

This, I see, is the voice that's always in the background – the one that's forever planning my next activity in the midst of this one. (*What will I do after I finish this draft? Will I post it right away? Will I take a break and review it later? If I take that break, how will I spend my time? A snack? A shower?* And so on, without end.) The voice begins to sound petty, needy, small; uneasiness courses through my body. I didn't realize I was quite this sick.

WILLIAM JAMES AND MENTAL ILLNESS

OCD AS A VARIETY OF RELIGIOUS EXPERIENCE

In his essay "The Reality of the Unseen," William James describes people who perceive gods or spirits just as vividly as they perceive objects directly in front of them. He quotes a fellow professor on his experiences with a mysterious, spirit-like presence.

James' colleague writes that for several nights, he felt the presence steal into his rooms, and in one case even grip his arm.

> I knew its presence far more surely than I have ever known the presence of any fleshly living creature...[T]he certainty that there in outward space there stood *something* was indescribably *stronger* than the ordinary certainty of companionship when we are in the close presence of ordinary living people. The something seemed close to me, and intensely more real than any ordinary perception.

James is asking us to understand something elemental to the study of religion. *Put aside your intellectual qualms about the existence of gods and spirits,* he seems to be saying. *Recognize that some people simply cannot not believe in them, for that is the nature of their experience.*

I have experiences of a very similar kind, albeit perhaps from a different source. I have OCD, or obsessive-compulsive disorder. OCD is characterized by intrusive thoughts that trigger intense fears. (In my case, these thoughts tend to have to do with physical risk – *I'm shaving the wrong way, and I'm going to cut my eyes. It'll be intensely painful, and I'll go blind. I won't be able to see or write, and my life will be miserable.*) These fears tempt sufferers to engage in rituals to try to make the thoughts go away. *(Put the razor down. Look in the mirror and decide exactly where you're going to place the blade on your cheek. Now pick it up and trace that pattern precisely.)*

Sometimes, the intrusive thoughts are so strong that I can't actually determine whether they're fears or memories. And sometimes, I become convinced that they *are* memories. In other words, I think that the things I'm afraid of happening have already happened. And I don't just *think* that way; I feel like I'm recalling how it happened – complete with vivid visuals and physical sensations.

In other words, there is something undeniable about these thoughts and feelings, which is why denying them doesn't work. (Thankfully, there are other ways of dealing with them.) In these moments, I 'know' that what I'm afraid of is true, just like you know you're reading this essay right now.

This is what James is getting at, I think. My experiences with OCD – shot through with magical thinking as they may be – are in some sense exactly parallel to certain kinds of religious experience. You can't talk me out of them, just like I could never talk an evangelical out of her conviction that she has a personal relationship with Jesus. And it's not because either of us is right or wrong. It's because we can't help believing what we believe.

LEARNING TO FALL APART

RITUAL IN BUDDHISM AND OCD

This essay was originally published in Aeon *(September, 2013).*

Our society likes to portray obsessive-compulsive disorder (OCD) as a cute quirk, a goofy, if irritating, eccentricity. It is not. For the person undergoing OCD experience, it is a form of mental terrorism.

This terrorism takes the form of what psychologists call 'intrusive thoughts' — unwanted, painful thoughts or images that invade one's consciousness, triggering profound fear and anxiety. This is the 'obsessive' part of OCD, and it can arise in even the most mundane circumstances. Sitting here typing, for example, I sometimes feel modest pain in my fingers, and my mind kicks into gear: *You're typing too much and causing permanent damage to your hands. Feel those little irritations at the second knuckle of your left ring finger? Those are the harbingers of arthritis. This is how it starts.*

All around this mental tickertape, tension begins to build — a tidal lift that threatens to drown me if I don't take immediate action. It's hard to overstate just how world-shrinkingly claustrophobic this can feel, or just how much I am tempted to do to make the feeling go away. And here's where the terrorists make their demands. *Type slower. Put your wrist guards on. Stop typing altogether. Then you won't have to feel this way.* These are the 'compulsions' — ritual behaviors meant to alleviate anxiety.

These rituals can take many forms. For some people, it's the stuff you see on TV — repeatedly checking to see if the door's locked, counting the letters in words until a particular total is reached, avoiding the cracks in the sidewalk. I've experienced some of this, but for me, invitations to ritualize tend to be more purely mental — to ruminate endlessly, to replay anxiety-producing scenarios until I find a way to view them that will dissipate my anxiety (which, of course, never happens). The common thread is the ritual, the promise that there's something repetitive and formalized that I can do to make things feel better.

Which brings us to religion. As in OCD, ritual plays a central role in all religious traditions. That's not to say, of course, that ritual plays exactly the *same* role in OCD and religion. After all, religious ritual is an enormous arena, a means of expression for nearly every human want, need, and desire. It would be way beyond hubris for me — a -31year-old whose experience of religious practice is largely limited to evangelical Christianity and Tibetan Buddhism — to pronounce on all of that.

In what follows, then, I'm going to quickly offer a few perspectives on religious ritual before turning my attention to what I know best – the Tibetan Buddhist tradition. I'll also share some of the ways that Tibetan Buddhist ritual and practice have helped me understand and respond to my OCD.

Some rituals are designed to help us "keep ourselves together." Others are designed to help us fall apart.

OCD rituals are the former. When intrusive thoughts begin their assault, it can feel as if my entire world is shattering in slow motion. My confidence – in my physical health, in the love of my friends and family, and in the idea that I'm a basically decent person – vanishes. I quickly fall into a powerful depression, a vortex into which only sadness and hopelessness are admitted. In such a state, the future appears as nothing but drawn-out misery – if I can lift my eyes off the ground at all.

In other words, OCD makes visible all of the implicit certainties and background assumptions that I rely on – and then destroys them. You can imagine the panicky floundering, the thrashing desperation– and above all, the willingness to reach for anything that looks remotely like a life raft.

Which, of course, is exactly how the ritual presents itself. *Just read over the essay one more time. It couldn't hurt to check the alarm again, could it? Why not drive at precisely the speed limit for the entire trip — that way, you couldn't possibly get pulled over.* In other words, the ritual doesn't necessarily come packaged *as* a ritual. Rather, it arrives in the form of perfectly calibrated pain medication, the oh-so-rational solution to my confusion and disarray. *Feeling a little groundless? Let's get you back on your feet.* OCD's rituals offer to restore the disrupted narrative of my life, to re-create a storyline in which all of my rollicking thoughts, feelings, and emotions can be integrated, and forward motion re-established.

As with OCD, so with religion. Many of the great anthropologists and sociologists of religion, including Émile Durkheim and Victor Turner, have pointed out the ways in which religious rituals serve to unite communities. But many religious rituals *attempt to unify the individual as well* – to restore a sense of coherence and continuity in our self-understanding. This can take many forms: purging oneself of immoral acts, restoring a damaged relationship with a deity, and so on. In the evangelical circles in which I grew up, great emphasis was put on 'getting right with God' — on being reborn in Christ and committing to 'walk with Him'. Doing so was a decisive act; it earned the believer a place among the saved and entry into Heaven.

Whatever their specific form, these practices and rituals promise that we will no longer be groundless, disintegrated. To help deliver on this promise, OCD and much religious ritual depend on the belief that there really is some kind of entity, some *thing* at the core of our identity. Hindus might call it *atman*; those raised in the West might prefer 'soul'. Whatever one calls it, many people firmly believe that somewhere within us there's a center, a seat of consciousness, a mental headquarters that processes experience and makes deliberate choices about how to move through the world.

Buddhism suggests that this is a profound mistake — that when we actually look for such an entity, a stable core to our being, there is simply nothing to be found. Unlike OCD, or the rituals of my evangelical childhood, Buddhist rituals work not because they teach us how to stay together, but because they show us how to fall apart.

Because the solid self is a fiction, it requires endless maintenance. We are constantly filtering our experience — excluding information, repressing our feelings, and ignoring our deep connections with other people — in order to defend and perpetuate a narrow understanding of ourselves. In other words, we're constantly deceiving ourselves about who and what we are.

Why, you might ask, would anyone engage in this kind of self-deception? The contemporary Tibetan Buddhist master Chögyam Trungpa Rinpoche suggests that we're afraid that when we look to the center of our own being, we won't find anything to hold on to. In his words, we're afraid that we don't exist.

According to traditional Buddhist teachings, being is marked by impermanence. Nothing — no experience, no thought, no feeling, no form of self-understanding, and certainly no physical body — lasts forever. And even when these things arise, they never stand alone. Rather, they are interdependent, composed of — and helping to compose — everything else.

The Abhidharma — a collection of traditional texts on Buddhist psychology — actually goes much further, describing how our own minds are composed of five basic elements (form, feeling, perception, concept, and consciousness). In other words, our minds are not the cognitive command rooms or centralized emotion-processing headquarters that we imagine them to be. Rather, the mind is a label that refers to nothing in and of itself, much like a crowd is nothing more than the coming together and interaction of individuals.

According to Buddhist psychology, we can actually witness the truth of these claims by observing how our own minds work. Buddhist ritual and practice seek to expose us to our own mental processes — to show us exactly how we create and perpetuate the illusions that keep us in such pain.

The centerpiece of Buddhist ritual and practice is, of course, meditation. There are a huge variety of meditative traditions and practices both within and beyond Buddhism, and new variations seem to appear regularly (particularly as the market for Eastern spirituality has exploded in the West). To be clear, then, I'm going to restrict my comments to traditional *shamatha-vipashyana* meditation as taught by Trungpa Rinpoche. (For the record, I've been a practitioner in his lineage for the past year and a half.)

In *shamatha-vipashyana*, the practitioner focuses on the outbreath, following it as it passes the tip of the nose and dissolves into space. Thoughts arise, of course, and when the practitioner notices that his attention has been diverted, he simply takes note and returns to the breath.

Over time, the practitioner begins to notice the sheer quantity of thoughts and feelings that his mind generates. He sees the way that these mental phenomena have a mysterious life of their own — that they arise from nowhere and then disappear again. He starts to realize that it is possible to see thoughts and feelings without judging them, reacting to them, or even identifying with them.

As this happens, the practitioner begins to notice some of the stories he tells himself. Some of these are big stories — about the kind of person he is, the 'meaning' of his life, and so on. Others are much smaller — his narrative about why he should buy this toothbrush rather than that one. But in both cases he starts to notice that these stories are simply composed of thoughts and feelings — like a string of popcorn on a Christmas tree. In other words, he recognizes that his stories about himself are made-up, too. (Practitioners of cognitive behavioral therapy — CBT — might find such insights familiar.)

As these insights arise, a kind of loosening occurs. Not only does the practitioner identify less with individual thoughts and feelings, but he also begins to rely less on particular ways of understanding himself. He feels less and less need to summarize his experience, to corral his raging flood of thoughts and feelings into a stable, permanent view of who he is. And as he starts to let go of his constant grasping after solidity, a fuller sense of who he is begins to emerge.

On a two-week solitary meditation retreat last month, I found out what happens when two types of ritual collide: my OCD, crafted to hold tight to a false self, and my Buddhist practice, designed to take it apart.

I was at Dorje Khyung Dzhong, a retreat center in a remote area of southern Colorado. DKD is comprised of eight retreat cabins strewn across 400 acres of otherwise-untouched wilderness. My teacher and another member of my meditation community were also there, in cabins about a half-mile from mine. Every three days or so, I would visit my teacher for an hour. Otherwise, we were each on our own.

The first week had been focused and intense. I opened and closed each day with a series of chants and offerings; in between, I spent long sessions in sitting and walking meditation. My mind was slowing down; there were even a few moments in between sessions when I realized that I wasn't thinking at all, and that nothing seemed to be missing.

On day six, though, I began to notice some pain in my knees. (I'd been nursing a low-grade knee injury for months, but things had been fine over the previous several days.) I couldn't tell whether this was OCD spinning a story about my choices and their consequences — I'd neglected to stretch before the painful sitting session — or whether the pain was 'real'. If it was an obsession, I certainly didn't want to give in and ritualize. On the other hand, I didn't want to be foolhardy with my body, especially with another week of retreat to go.

At some point, the rising mental tension simply forced a choice. I traded my meditation stool for a chair, hoping that this would put less pressure on my knees.

Whatever the truth of the matter, I had conceded some ground – and this made it all the easier it to concede again. I scrapped sitting meditation entirely, added more walking sessions, and introduced laying meditation.

Over the next few days, the pattern intensified. Even walking meditation 'hurt', so I limited myself to laying practice. I scanned my body for the faintest signs of discomfort; when I sensed the slightest twitch or twinge, my mind would flood with tension.

Even sitting at the table to eat or read became unmanageable. I constructed an elaborate contraption out of pillows and chairs, a form of improvised traction that I hoped would suspend me above my anxieties for a few minutes at a time. Just getting situated required a delicate set of bodily movements, each of which necessitated readjusting the equipment. I had built myself a prison for one.

It had become clear: my OCD rituals were preventing me from undertaking the Buddhist rituals I had come on retreat to practice. Staying had begun to feel masochistic, and in consultation with my teacher, I decided to leave.

This last retreat may have been more than I was ready for. What it did not do, though, was undermine my faith in the value of meditation practice. OCD may have gotten the upper hand, but it's been getting the upper hand for decades. It takes time to slow down and reverse such deeply entrenched patterns.

OCD often feels like a *Choose Your Own Adventure* novel, except that all the choices suck and all the adventures hurt. As I've begun to learn through Buddhist study and ritual, however, those 'choices' are illusory, and there's no one being hurt. In fact, there's no one there at all. The attempt to attain pleasure or avoid pain, to stay consistent with a storyline, to ensure some kind of outcome, to *be somebody* — this is what causes so much suffering.

That's a hard message to hear, in part because our culture places such a heavy emphasis on the construction of an integrated self with a coherent storyline. We are trained to believe that deep down, there is some kind of solid, stable bedrock to our identity, some unshakable foundation that provides us with the capacity to control significant portions of our experience – to be 'true' to ourselves, to be who we 'really are.' Much religious ritual is designed to reinforce this view — to convince us that it's possible to keep ourselves together, and to provide a method that promises to help us do so. And while there are important differences, OCD and its rituals are built on a similar worldview.

But that worldview isn't true. It isn't possible to keep ourselves together, because we aren't one coherent thing. Instead, we are a kind of flux, a series of patterns and surprises, inextricably interwoven into the larger field of phenomena that we call reality. Which means that we can't really let ourselves fall apart either, because we were never together in the first place. What we can do, though, is recognize these truths and learn to be at peace with them.

Of course, it's one thing to talk or write this way. It's another thing entirely to know these truths in your body, at the level of instinct. And here, according to Buddhism, is where meditation practice is essential. By sitting alone with ourselves, and by seeing what our minds are always doing, we begin to rediscover space, to remember that it's possible to step off the conveyor belt and watch it go by.

WHAT OCD HAS TAUGHT ME ABOUT
BUDDHISM (AND VICE VERSA)

A version of this essay appeared in Shambhala Sun
(November, 2014).

In the first of the *Lotus Sutra* allegories, a man must convince his children to put aside their toys in order to escape a burning house. To do so, the man contrives an even more tempting set of playthings – the three 'chariots' of the Buddhist teachings.

Like almost everyone, I spend most of my time in the grip of ignorance, attachment, and aversion. And like almost everyone, I require the rescue we see in the *Lotus Sutra*. But in one sense, my challenges feel different than the average citizen of samsara.

I have obsessive-compulsive disorder, or OCD. As I've written elsewhere,

> the cycle typically begins with what psychologists call 'intrusive thoughts' – unwanted, painful thoughts or images that invade one's consciousness, triggering profound fear and anxiety. This is the 'obsessive' part of OCD, and it can arise in even the most mundane circumstances. Sitting here typing, for example, I sometimes feel modest pain in my fingers, and my mind kicks into gear: *You're typing too much and causing permanent damage to your hands. Feel those little irritations*

at the second knuckle of your left ring finger? Those are the harbingers of arthritis. This is how it starts.

All around this mental tickertape, tension begins to build — a tidal lift that threatens to drown me if I don't take immediate action. It's hard to overstate just how world-shrinkingly claustrophobic this can feel, or just how much I am tempted to do to make the feeling go away. And here's where the mental terrorists make their demands. *Type slower. Put your wrist guards on. Stop typing altogether. Then you won't have to feel this way.* These are the 'compulsions' — ritual behaviors meant to alleviate anxiety.

This process is immensely confusing, in part because I don't have a handle on the source of my intrusive thoughts. Some of them, after all, bear at least a tenuous relationship to reality – repetitive stress injury does happen – even if the fears I feel and the consequences I imagine are wildly out of proportion to the situation at hand.

Other times, however, the intrusive thoughts part company with reality entirely. While putting my glasses on, for example, I sometimes imagine that I've inadvertently scratched my eye with my fingernails. My mind quickly generates a whole host of potential repercussions – an inability to read or write, and ultimately, blindness itself.

Terrified, I immediately scan my memory. *Do I remember any contact between my fingers and my eyes? Did I feel any pain?* Unfortunately, the fear flooding my system distorts everything, and I find myself unable to recall events clearly from even a moment before.

In an effort to sort through the fog, I sometimes find myself visualizing what it *would* have felt like to scratch my eyes. I sense my fingers converging on my eyes, feel the pressure of contact, undergo the cutting sensation. Unfortunately, this only confuses things further. Now, I have the memories I was looking for, but I can't discern whether they 'really happened' or whether I made them up. Memory and imagination blur, and I'm left even more anxious than before.

For me, living with OCD means having a mind which fabricates events that never happened and projects consequences that never will. On a day-to-day level, then, the greatest source of suffering in my life isn't a refusal to leave a burning house. It's my desire to flee a house that isn't burning at all.

I was diagnosed at 18, and for the next year-and-a-half, I did my damnedest to deny that the diagnosis meant anything. I was already spending huge portions of my day wrapped up in obsessive-compulsive cycles; the last thing I wanted was to devote even more time to therapy. Eventually, though, the pain became so constant that I conceded.

I began taking Lexapro, an antidepressant, and tried out a series of psychologists. Some of these therapists wanted to chat, to relate with my experiences by sharing similar stories of their own. Others tried to examine and deconstruct the unrealistic assumptions that fueled my fears. The best of the bunch – Dr. B. – did the least overt psychologizing: he simply provided a space in which I could pour out the almost impossibly concentrated anxieties that had accumulated throughout the week.

I left many of my conversations with Dr. B feeling ever so slightly hopeful, as if I'd taken the first creaky steps toward resurrection. The trouble was that it was just a feeling; I hadn't learned any techniques to sustain my momentum. Over the next several days, the effects would wear off, and I would be sucked right back into the vortex.

About five years ago, I volunteered to participate in a research study on OCD. In exchange, I received several months of free treatment in a form of cognitive behavioral therapy known as exposure and response prevention (ERP). In ERP, the OCD sufferer exposes himself to the stimuli that trigger his fears and then deliberately refrains from the compulsions that arise. The idea is that as the sufferer leans into his fears rather than reacting to them, the triggering stimuli begin to lose their power.

During the first few months of treatment, I spent several hours each day conducting a variety of different exposures. Sometimes, I would write a paragraph like the following that captured a particular set of fears.

I've recklessly and carelessly scratched my eyes. As a result, they'll get worse and worse. I won't be able to read, write, or do any of the things I enjoy, and I'll be miserable. And there's nothing I can do about it.

I would then sit and repeat the paragraph out loud until my anxiety diminished to a level my therapist and I had agreed upon. Other times, I would create shorter versions – just a sentence, or even a phrase – and repeat them in my head.

I also conducted *in vivo* exposures – impromptu responses to fears whenever and wherever they happened to arise. Riding the train from Brooklyn to my therapist's office on 168th St., for example, I sometimes became afraid that I was inducing tumors by leaning my head against the vibrating subway car wall. In these instances – when I could summon my courage – I would hold my head against the jittery metal for an extra five or ten or 30 seconds, allowing myself to feel the full weight of my fear and refusing to respond.

I never liked doing exposure work, and not just because it was painful. Mostly, it felt tedious, and I imagined that I ought to be doing something more interesting than practicing getting in and out of bed. But the theory made sense to me, and the practice generated immediate results: I noticed that I was managing daily tasks a bit more easily and feeling a little less overwhelmed.

When I began meditating, I thought I would continue both practices in parallel. Very quickly, though, I noticed what felt like a subtle tension between them. This was strange; from a certain vantage point, ERP and meditation seem deeply complementary. After all, both are driven by the understanding that thoughts are just thoughts – and that the more time we sit with them, the less we will mistake them for reality, and the less reactive we will become.

The difference – or so it seemed at the time – is that ERP is goal-oriented: it aims at these results directly. Meditation – at least in my lineage – doesn't work this way. One doesn't plop down on the cushion and say, "Now I'll work on becoming less reactive." In fact, one doesn't practice in order to *get* anything at all. One simply sits, trusting that the only route to sanity is to stop trying to do things all the time and simply spend time with oneself.[1]

Over time, the tension grew. Despite knowing that my exposure work

---

1   It's certainly true that meditation practitioners often identify less and less with their thoughts over time. But this tends to be a byproduct of practice; as soon as we start treating it like a prize to be won, it whisps away.

often led to a deep sense of resilience and empowerment, I continued to dread it. I can't claim that I lost faith in the techniques, and I certainly can't claim that they weren't working. It was simpler than that: my exposure exercises felt too much like the rest of my life – yet another arena in which I was perpetually trying to improve myself, to get away from my experience in the here and now. For a while, I discontinued ERP. I wasn't sure about the wisdom of this decision, but I was too exhausted to do otherwise.

Recently, though, I've come back around. My energy has returned, but more importantly, I've begun to grasp ERP at a subtler level. Understood properly, ERP isn't about escapism, and it isn't inconsistent with meditation. In fact, one might think of it as a very specific *kind* of meditation.

Meditation is about facing our own minds and encountering whatever arises. As a result, there's often a certain randomness to meditation experience: who knows what will pop up? ERP, on the other hand, is about acknowledging that certain thoughts and feelings arise more often than others, and that it can be prudent to prepare ourselves for their arrival.

OCD is an overactive alarm system, a jumpy nightwatchman. Intrusive thoughts trigger a powerful fear response, and because our bodies are built to take fear seriously – to treat it as a sign that danger is afoot – I find myself believing my thoughts and wanting to react. (This is one of OCD's profound ironies: intrusive thoughts set off profound chain reactions precisely because they're so outlandish.)

As my anxiety spikes past the red line, I feel pressed to make a choice. Do I continue with whatever I was doing and lean into the fear (knowing, at some level, that this is OCD at work)? Or do I give into my compulsions in an effort to make the fear subside (knowing, at some level, that this will strengthen the cycle in the long term)?

It's even more complicated than that, however, because the fears don't arise in isolation. Rather, they tend to activate entire networks of other fears. I'll be cutting vegetables for dinner, and it will occur to me that my attention has drifted. I'll wonder: *While I was daydreaming, did I accidentally press the knife blade against a tendon in my finger? Have I cut myself?* If I see no signs of damage, I might ask, *Was the damage more subtle than that? Have I weakened myself in a way that will make future injury more likely?*

In these moments, part of me wants to push through the fears, to clang pots and pans defiantly. Another part believes that I've already screwed up, and that I can only make things worse by acting cavalier. I might try to split the difference and continue cooking in a spirit of moderation, moving objects around without being too brash or too tender. But the sweet spot will elude me, and everything I do will feel like a drastic mistake.

Meanwhile, my kitchen – so innocuous just a moment before – will become the site of a thousand old worries, all blooming into new and vigorous life. I'll remember my concern about repetitive stress injury, and I'll begin to feel afraid to touch anything. I'll consider walking out of the room, but I'll recall old tremblings about walking into walls and damaging my eyes. I'll shift my footing, only to summon a million voices screaming about disintegrating knees. Eventually, I'll feel completely boxed in, and I'll find myself staring – first at the handle of a pot or pan, and then blankly – swamped by the gravity of the situation.

When I fall into this fearful place, I see danger and consequences in every direction. It feels impossible to make good choices, because the strike zone is so vanishingly small. And so I spend a good portion of my day trying to ensure that I won't fall into this place – avoiding everyday situations, weighing my word choices incredibly carefully, pausing and breathing when my mind starts to spin too quickly. If OCD is an overactive alarm system, I do my damnedest not to trip it – or rather, to trip myself. For years now, I've been afraid to be afraid.

Because OCD is so terrifying, frustrating, and depressing, it's also shot through with a desire for security, for permanent guarantees against suffering. Every day, I feel all kinds of things I don't want to feel, and it's the easiest thing in the world to invent rules and guidelines in the hopes that I won't have to feel them again.

To say it in a slightly more Buddhist valence: OCD is built on the premise that control is possible, and that there's someone there – some kind of "self" – to do the controlling. But as the *dharma* points out – and as meditation reveals – this just isn't true.

I study and practice in the lineage of Chögyam Trungpa Rinpoche. (My teacher, Lee Ray, was one of his students.) Within our *sangha*, many of us joke that we've each come to Buddhism after trying everything else. And there's some truth to that; after all, meditation forces us to spend time with ourselves, to see what's going on inside. And like most people, that's the last thing we want to do.

But there's also a deep irony in our use of the word 'trying' – one that marks the difference between the *dharma* and just about every philosophy, religion, or form of self-help that I've seen. The Buddha's teachings are clear: most of our suffering is generated precisely because we are constantly trying to be something other than what we are. Trungpa Rinpoche talked about this as the work of ego – that if we only push harder and exercise more discipline, we'll get exactly what we want out of life: more experiences we like, an ability to steer clear of the ones we don't, and a pleasant, consistent storyline about who we are.

These, of course, are the snares of *samsara* – the mirages we spend our whole lives chasing. And there's only one way that we can begin to see them for the traps they are: by practicing meditation.

For me, meditation has been a revolution, a way of becoming acquainted with the basic spaciousness within. OCD, after all, admits of no space – it is a perpetual hemming-in, the spiky descending ceiling in *Indiana Jones and the Temple of Doom*.

When I began practicing about two years ago, then, I thought I had found a way out of my incessant battles with OCD. Finally, an hour or two each day in which I didn't have to take my thoughts and feelings so seriously! In which my entire task was simply to breathe and let everything go. *In which there wasn't any way to screw up.*

I should have expected no such reprieve. After all, OCD tends to target and undermine whatever I care about most at a given time. And so it threatened practice, too. As I begin meditating more regularly, the intrusive thoughts mounted their counterattack. *What if I was practicing incorrectly, and whatever insights I'd had paled in comparison to the ones I could have if only I'd practiced with more discipline or better form? What if I was taking the wrong attitude toward practice – that instead of working to erode ego and escape the tethers of conceptual thinking, I was chasing new forms of what Trungpa called "spiritual materialism"? And what if I was overdoing it physically? What if, out of the depth of my grasping, I was on the way to injuring my knees and making it impossible to meditate?*

In other words, OCD did what it always does: it escalated, raising the tension to a point just beyond what I feel like I can handle. It issued ultimatums: *in order for your life to be tolerable, it needs to look a very particular way.* And it spat out threats: *if you can't make your life look that way, the abyss awaits.*

My samsaric mind very much wanted to take the bait, and on many days, it did. Thankfully, though, I had a new resource: the *dharma* itself. Through study and practice, I was no longer quite so convinced that the only way to conduct this conversation was on OCD's terms. Yes, perhaps my life would need to take a particular shape, but it wasn't clear to me that I was in charge of shaping it – and the perhaps the form it took would have nothing to do with what I envisioned.

I'm always resistant when people try to suggest that there might be an "upside" to OCD. Yes, I am meticulous, and yes, an attention to detail is useful in the world. But OCD differs from meticulousness precisely because it goes well beyond the point of usefulness – in other words, because it's out of tune with reality.

Weirdly, though, a familiarity with neurotic thinking might be its own advantage. After all, the basic Buddhist view suggests that we're all deeply confused and wildly neurotic. And, at least in one sense, this didn't come as a shock to me. In fact, it was very reason I had come to practice.

Of course, like anyone new to the Buddhist view, I've been surprised to discover just how deep my neuroses go. It isn't just my weird fears or spastic compulsions; it's a basic way of being in the world that is dominated by the three *kleshas* – ignorance, attachment, and aversion. In other words, OCD may be a special species of confusion, but it's only an additional layer on top of the madness we all share.

Bent in half, sobs moving through my chest like waves, it's easy to imagine that I'm uniquely disabled. More: it's easy to believe that my suffering is pointless, nothing more than the short-circuiting of a poorly wired brain. And this belief – that this isn't real life, and that real life is elsewhere – only compounds the pain.

But practice shows me something else – that along with my neuroses, wisdom is always arising as well. That every experience – no matter how horrific – contains some kind of teaching. And that tallying experiences up like this – into 'good' and 'bad', 'helpful' or 'unhelpful' – isn't particularly useful, anyway. Experience isn't trying to sell us something, and it doesn't owe us anything either. It simply is, and the more we practice, the more we become capable of living our lives – and feeling what we feel – without judgment. We start to be tenderer with ourselves, and underneath our suffering, and we sense the existence of a deeper truth about who we are – a basic openness, goodness, and compassion. A flow of easy awareness that doesn't judge, grasp, and or even want much for itself. OCD may be a Technicolor film festival of worry, but it's also a blinking neon arrow pointing toward truth.

William James wrote that religions begin with our sense that something is basically wrong – with life, with the world, with existence itself. OCD starts there too. But OCD, like most religions, attempt to solve this problem – to make that feeling go away. Buddhism, on the other hand, suggests that the problem itself is an illusion, the product of mistaken conceptual thinking, and that quelling suffering is a matter of practicing our way to a fuller and fuller realization of that truth.

Descriptions of enlightenment are hard to come by, but here's one I like. According to Dzongsar Khyentse Rinpoche, to be enlightened is to be free of obsessions. Most of the time, I feel almost parodically far from that ideal. Thanks to practice, though, I have my moments.

OCD: A WAY OF DISTRACTING MYSELF FROM SOMETHING EVEN SCARIER

Buddhism makes much of the ceaseless stream of thoughts and feelings that course through our minds. I can certainly identify, but there are times when it feels like the stream dries up, when I'm occupied by just a single thought for long periods. The thought itself can fluctuate, but it's invariably of the obsessive variety. It invades, occupies, colonizes, and turns me slowly on a spit.

OCD is a special kind of torture. But as Stephen Batchelor reminds me, in some ways it is nothing more than another technique our minds have dreamed up to steal us away from basic, moment-to-moment awareness. "Much of the time we are driven by a relentless and insistent surge of impulses," Batchelor writes.

> "We notice this in quiet moments of reflection, but usually just get carried along on the crest of its wave. Until, that is, we crash once more onto the rocks of recriminatory self-consciousness, and from there into moods and depressions." (*Buddhism Without Beliefs*, 58)

This is exactly how my OCD often plays out. I spend a great deal of time trying to anticipate and avoid situations that might trigger obsessive-compulsive cycles. Inevitably, I get distracted and drift off (or simply get sick of my self-imposed sentry duty and let down my guard as an act of protest). When I return to awareness and realize that I've failed to keep watch, I become terrified that something awful has happened in the interim; usually, I imagine it's exactly the thing I was supposed to be watching out for. Cue the recriminatory self-consciousness and depression.

I'm not suggesting that my fear-driven vigilance is anything like awareness, of course. I'm saying the opposite: OCD itself is a way of distracting myself from a more direct engagement with the unpredictability of my experience. It is a way of prejudging that experience, of dividing it into 'acceptable' and 'unacceptable' categories and demanding that I find a way to live only in the former. Which is impossible, of course – hence my inevitable failure.

True awareness, however, doesn't seek to build barriers against experience. As Batchelor writes:

> Awareness is a process of deepening self-acceptance. It is neither a cold, surgical examination of life nor a means of becoming perfect. Whatever it observes, it embraces. The light of awareness will doubtless illuminate things we would prefer not to see. And this may entail a descent into what is forbidden, repressed, denied. (59)

OCD likes to fancy itself a last line of defense, a protector of the realm. It is not. It is a cowering, shivering little boy playing dress-up, a bully who picks fights with older kids because he'd rather have the shit kicked out of him than spend one more minute alone with himself.

OCD IS A FULL-TIME JOB

Most of the time, I forget that I have OCD.

This might sound strange: how do you lose touch with the biggest, most destructive thing in your life?

Well I don't, exactly – but I also don't understand it as a disease. Instead, I operate under the belief that I'm "normal," and that I'm just sort of screwing up all the time. Like that tagline from *Girls*: almost getting it kind of together. But never quite.

You'd think that fourteen years after diagnosis, and twelve years after beginning both therapy and medication, the reality of my condition would have sunk in. That after decades living under a siege of self-cannibalizing thoughts and fears, I'd have come to understand that life is a little different for me.

But OCD is paradoxical that way. On one hand, there's no mistaking the pain it causes. On the other hand, that pain is completely intangible, composed entirely of illusions. *What's wrong with me again?* That I sometimes have completely unrealistic thoughts which generate unbelievably powerful fears. *But none of that is real – so why is this so painful again?*

This is a perpetual mindfuck.

Most mornings, I make a plan for the day. I do so to give myself a sense of predictability – so that no matter how bad I feel, I have a path to follow, a path that's bigger than my feelings. So that the feelings don't become too dominant and I don't become too reactive.

Deviating from the plan, then, can feel really consequential. The other morning, I altered my routine so that I could download a book onto my Kindle before heading out. (I'd been feeling lonely, and I thought a new novel might be a nice reprieve.) It turned out that the book wasn't available, and I found myself disappointed. In that space, the prospect of going out and starting another solo day felt too bleak, too self-punishing. I found myself clicking over into email, hoping to tamp down the loneliness. And I immediately felt guilty – that I was being reactive, and I shouldn't have changed my plans. A nasty swarm of intrusive thoughts began making their way into the room.

Why now? After all, I'd already altered my plan once. And while doing so had made me feel a bit nervous, it was only the second change that sent shrapnel spinning though my mind.

It took me a few hours, but I finally discerned the difference. In the first instance – the decision to download a book – I'd been sorting through confusion, trying to discover what I actually felt and wanted (as opposed to just enacting my normal routine out of a desire for security). In the second instance, though, I already *had* clarity – I knew I was feeling disappointment, and I just didn't like it. So I tried to run away.

Zen teacher Barry Magid talks about our ineluctable need for love and warmth. Seeking out the book was my way of extending myself that warmth. And when I failed, the need was still there, so I sought company in my inbox. The fact that I felt so guilty about indulging that need has helped me see something: that I deeply distrust the notion of need itself. For a couple of years now, I've interpreted Buddhist teachings to mean that dependency is equivalent to grasping, and is therefore unhealthy. So I've done my best to recognize the areas of my life where I feel dependent, and to whittle down my tendency to self-indulge. A progressive asceticism.

Recently, a buddy suggested that this mix of motives was at work in my political writing, too – that I feel a need to speak out, but that I feel guilty about it. I'm not sure he's entirely right, but I do think there's something there – I very much want to avoid speaking reactively, out of anger or aggression. But – as with most people, perhaps – those impulses are rampant in me. So I spend a lot of my time pausing, checking in on my feelings, trying to discern what's moving me to speak. On one hand, this feels necessary; I don't want to just spew my inner garbage all over the place, and I certainly don't want to hurt people. On the other hand, it sometimes feels as if my vigilance has *itself* become reactive – a fear of doing the 'wrong' thing, of spontaneity, of losing control.

Ultimately, that's what all of my daily self-scheduling is about. I plan my day because I don't trust that I'll be able to handle emotional surprises, nor the uncertainty and groundlessness that arise between activities. More simply, I don't trust myself to respond appropriately to the thoughts or feelings that might come up. My schedule becomes a dividing wall, then – clean streets and clockwork on one side, confusion and disorder on the other. That's the idea, anyway. But of course, it doesn't work.

I lie in bed with a tickle in my nose. I vow not to scratch it for 20 minutes, until the end of the podcast I'm listening to. Impulses go to war. On one side, spontaneity (that hardest-to-argue-with of the virtues). On the other side, my desire not to be overcome by compulsive spontaneity.

And lately, I've been overcome quite often. Because as I've sought to put aside my schedule and respond more fully to my impulses, I've gotten a little carried away. I find myself responding to every feeling – constantly readjusting myself on my motorbike seat, looking up from my book every time I feel even slightly fatigued, getting up from the keyboard to pee every twenty minutes (and then discovering I don't have to). And I've come to wonder – if I become too spontaneous, will I lose the capacity for discipline entirely? Will I be unable to sustain any activity for more than a few seconds? Will life spin down into a Pig Pen-cloud of confusion?

Some mornings I sit in cafes, reading things that leave me smiling or crunching up my face, pre-tears. I look up at the walls or out at the boughs overhanging the boulevards.

My friend Jenna tells me that she doesn't know what she's doing. Not relationship-wise or career-wise or in any other specific sense, but just generally – moment-to-moment.

I don't know what I'm doing either, J. There is either something inside, waiting to come out, or there isn't. But whatever's there is hidden. So I sit here, learning how to live, or learning nothing at all.

My friend Mike reminds me that beliefs are simply habits, thoughts we think over and over. An example: I want nothing other than to write, but I worry that an injured finger will stand in my way. The instrument of my liberation, contorted by OCD into the instrument of my torment.

About ten years ago, I fractured my right ring finger ever so slightly. I had bought a pair of rollerblades and – too excited to wait until I got to the park – I strapped them on in my densely packed city neighborhood. A hill took me, and – afraid to let myself fall – I picked up speed, slicing the 18-inch gap between a cop and a motorist, dancing with luck between cars coming off a green light. I became aware: *you could have died.* There but by the grace of God? But no God would protect a person so careless and let others perish.

In the park, I fell.

I would recover. Three years later, though, I began feeling strain in that finger as I typed. I saw a physical therapist, and then another, and then another. I handled objects gingerly, learned stretches and exercises, bought dictation software and a headset. To this day, I wear wrist braces when I type.

How likely is it that this injury remains? It's a strange limbo: not painful enough to be totally incapacitating, but not nothing enough to leave me be. Just bothersome, oil in the water, piss in the stew. *What is this pain, exactly? Just a scratch on the fender? Or a sign of things to come?* I never get clarity, but the question remains.

But the question is a mistake. The world doesn't work like that – things are or they aren't, but they don't float, permanently, at precisely eye-level. There is only one thing on earth that tracks our eyes and shadows our hearts in this way, and that is fear – that perpetual shapeshifter, that shameless opportunist.

OCD involves a great deal of magical thinking, and one of its tricks is convincing me of near-impossible coincidences. An example: while snowboarding two months ago, I faceplanted off a jump. On the surface, nothing too dramatic – just a busted lip. Inside, though, I was shaken to the core. I had fallen out of the air and landed directly on one of the areas of my body that I worry about most – my mouth and teeth. It felt like a Life Event – a BC/AD watershed.

Since then, I've developed an increasingly firm belief that my face is actually misshapen – that my mouth, chin, and jaw have been pressed backwards, leaving my oversized nose to dominate even more prime facial real estate. And it's not just a belief. It actually looks this way to me in the mirror.

Now, who knows? Maybe this really happened. But consider – for that to be true, it would have to be possible for me to reorient my face without breaking any bones. I'd have to have moved things just enough for me to notice, but not enough for anyone else to detect. (Boxers rarely find this sweet spot.) Oh! And I'd have to have done all this subtle-but-decisive facial reconstruction in precisely the area of my body that I've worried about most over the years. A true miracle.

Consciousness dawns, vaguely. I'm coming up from somewhere deep in the REM cycle; it's not even clear that I'm awake.

First thought: *you're definitely up. Not gonna fall back asleep. So don't malinger – out of bed with you.*

My "no malingering" rule isn't moral, really. (I have a heaping dose of Protestant work ethic in me, but that's not what this is.) I often wind up in painful struggles when I start negotiating with myself about whether to get out of bed, so I've created a little heuristic: if I detect that spark, that inner certainty that I'm not going to fall back asleep, then it's time to get up.

But I'm also tired as fuck, and it's weird to feel obligated to get up when I'm this drowsy. I go to the bathroom to pee and then come back. *Maybe I'll lay down again, try to let this rising noise settle, see if I can detect the spark a little more clearly.*

But wait: am I now acting on obsessive doubt, refusing the truth I've already recognized and compulsively searching for further certainty? If so, then I'm violating my central rule: don't compulse, no matter how strong the temptation. The tension starts to accumulate again, and I can feel it pooling in my fingers. I lay for a moment, but I can't make out anything in the murk – all I see is that this struggle is going to continue until I get out of bed and start my day. So I do.

It helps to talk to myself. For a long time, I thought of self-talk as just another form of struggle – a continuation of internal politics by other means. Recently, though, I've been giving it a spin.

It feels useful, because we speak much more slowly than we think. (I like typing for the same reason.) I rarely resolve anything internally, because all of the voices are shouting over each other. With speech, though, only one voice gets to speak at a time. I'd have predicted that this would just prolong the debate, but the pace somehow seems to set the tone: articulating one thought at a time communicates a kind of sanity that no individual thought ever does. Which is perhaps why spending time with other people is such a massive relief, too – it's necessarily slower than living in my own mental stock car race.

I never lose track of time, because nothing lasts very long for me. My anxiety means that it takes a great deal of energy to sustain effort for even short periods – to read a few chapters of a novel, to type up some notes. My mind is like an OPEC analyst – always monitoring internal energy reserves, calculating likely outputs, hedging against risk. In other words, I'm forever making a profound mistake: I believe that in order to get what I need, I must live in the present and the future simultaneously.

OCD capitalizes on this mistake. I've been noticing recently that the pain only seems to let up once it's dragged me through the mud and wrung me completely dry – once it's outlasted me, and I've resigned myself to the idea that it's going to be permanently semi-shitty from here on out. Once I've given up hope. Or perhaps once I've given up on controlling the future.

OCD AND THE ART OF
MOTORBIKE MAINTENANCE

When I came home from my first stint living in Vietnam, people frequently asked me what my favorite thing about the experience had been.

"Motorbikes," I would say.

It felt a little silly – thin, even superficial. Five months in a (nominally) Communist country with 1000+ years of fascinating history (including a torturous war with my own country), and the most important thing had been something I could have done on spring break back home?

But it was true then and, after spending a couple of weeks in Saigon over Christmas, it remains true now.

It isn't just the thrill – I'm sure there are a million ways to jack more adrenaline into your system (though accelerating through gaps in traffic is a hell of a rush). It's deeper than that: riding helps quiet the ongoing assault of intrusive thoughts crashing into my mind, because it requires a kind of concentration that leaves very little mental space for anything else. It's a thousand quick decisions and no time to revisit them, because you have to make another one *now, now, now, now.*

There are lots of things in this world that require concentration, of course, but almost all of them are optional. This is part of why I find it so difficult to run long distances or read Continental philosophy – I know that very little is at stake, and that I can bail out at any moment.

Activities that involve other people – team sports, say – can be more helpful, if only because bailing out means bailing on others. Still, though, I'm often very aware of the game's ultimate triviality. I don't *need* to be playing, so it's easy for me to imagine everything that might go wrong – a twisted ankle, an exacerbated shoulder injury – and preemptively blame myself for taking unnecessary risks.

This is how OCD tends to work for me – by treating everything I want as decadent, and by equating pleasure and whimsy with foolhardiness, the disease strips life down to its skinniest bones.

But what happens when there's nothing left to ruin? No matter how badly I feel, I still have to eat, to sleep, to move my body. I still have to get around, and when I'm in a place like Saigon, there aren't many alternatives. Public transportation is incomprehensible to me; walking is absurd; little 125cc Hondas are the only option. It's just what's done here. The paradox of choice, sliced through.

I realize that the goal of the best OCD therapy isn't to get away from painful thoughts – it's to become more accustomed and less reactive to them. Amen to all of that – I'm not recommending that we hunt for more effective ways to distract ourselves from pain. But it is nice to break the tension every now and again.

OCD loves options, loves to turn a debate into a dilemma. But when there's nothing to debate, there's no dilemma; and without a dilemma, there's nothing to ruin. Things just have to happen. Necessity breeds freedom. Errands become fun. The breeze hits my chest as I lean into a turn.

DOCTOR WITHOUT BORDERS

A BIZARRE FIRST BRUSH WITH PSYCHIATRY

A waiting my first appointment with a psychiatrist, I look down and notice a brochure. "There is no such thing as mental illness anymore," it reads. "There are only physical illnesses of the brain."

Anymore? I wonder. The brochure suggests that mental illnesses were once real, but no longer – now, they're just illusions. I see the point that the author is trying to make – that we don't need to mystify mental illness, and that addressing it is simply a matter of biochemistry. But I'm troubled by the metaphysical mistake: if mental illness isn't real now, then it never was.

The language seems exuberant, huckster-ish. I wonder who might have said such a thing – some large, conservative, professional organization, I hope. Perhaps their marketing people just got carried away.

I look closer. The quote is from the doctor I'm about to see.

On the wall above his couch hangs a framed poster – a blue silhouette in four poses, beginning in the fetal position and slowly rising to its feet. The picture has a Futurist, Ayn Rand feel – a schematic, angular optimism that I doubt bears much resemblance to real life.

The doctor indicates a seat next to his desk and prompts me for a history of my symptoms. He wants incredibly granular detail, and as he scratches out notes, I take him in. He is somehow both slight and dumpy, pants hiked up over a cantalouped front-butt. His face is clean-shaven, save for two rebellious copses of long, wiry whiskers. An extremely long fingernail forms the terminus of his left pointer finger.

By this time, I've seen enough therapists to know that wisdom doesn't always come in pretty vessels. But the doctor's appearance isn't just unattractive; it smells of ignorance, details overlooked, neglect. The brochure floats back into view.

By the end of that first session, we were talking drugs. I would begin with 10 milligrams of Celexa, a selective serotonin reuptake inhibitor (SSRI).

The doctor explained that serotonin is a neurotransmitter, and that its release is associated with wellbeing and happiness. In people with depression, however, synapses in the brain tend to reabsorb serotonin too quickly. As a result, I wasn't experiencing many good feelings, and when I did, they didn't last very long. In my depressed mood, I was finding it increasingly difficult to deal with the onslaught of OCD-driven intrusive thoughts.

By using an SSRI, the doctor explained, we would cut off something like the bottom 10% of my emotional range, and I wouldn't be as likely to fall into such despair. *Think of the medicine like scaffolding,* he suggested: by providing a supportive platform, the drug would help make it possible for me to change my mental habits.

Unfortunately, he added, the medicine would also slice off the top 10% of my feelings – my most joyful and ecstatic moments. I'm sure I asked him why the medicine worked this way, but I'm also sure that I didn't feel much resistance. I was in far too much pain to worry about a slight reduction in the intensity of good feelings that didn't appear very often anyway.

My decision to try medicine hadn't come quickly. In my typical OCD way, I had fretted about it for months: *How long had these things been around? Did we really know enough about the long-term effects? What if taking them ended up solving one problem by causing another? What if I gave myself cancer – then how would I feel? Maybe better to just soldier on.* As with my decision to see a therapist a year and a half before, though, the daily pain-grind eventually wore me down.

The first time I filled my prescription, I still wasn't sure I would go ahead. I took the bottles home, placed them on the counter, and stared at them for a moment. And then I realized that I'd already made my decision.

As with anything fearsome, ingesting pills seemed like a big deal until I did it. It was like being afraid of flying and getting on a plane for the first time: fear no longer made any sense. Things were in motion, processes underway.

People ask if the drugs make a difference, and I don't know what to tell them. I've been taking medicine for nearly twelve years now, and I don't remember what things felt like before.

It was hard to tell even at the outset. At the beginning, I would meet with my psychiatrist every month or so. Each time, he would ask a battery of questions about the frequency and intensity of my anxieties. I found these questions profoundly – even existentially – confusing: *How often was 'sometimes'? What was a 'moderate' amount of pain? And what would happen if I provided answers that didn't track my feelings perfectly?* (To provide me compass points, the doctor would sometimes tell me how I had answered the question at hand on my previous visit. I was grateful, though I wondered whether this was cheating and would skew the results.)

Each of the possible answers correlated with a point value. After we finished his questionnaire, the doctor would add them up and compare the total to my previous visit. Tiny changes meant a lot to him; if I scored a 29 on one visit and a 27 the next – lower was better – he took that to mean that the medicine was working.

I don't think he was wrong, exactly; without the numbers, I wouldn't have been able to tell whether I was making any headway at all. My mind was a tight and constricted place – one panicky, claustrophobic day indistinguishable from the next. Sure, things might not feel much different day to day, but what did I know? I was trying to differentiate between shades of black.

On one level, then, I appreciated having an outside perspective. But I didn't trust his self-satisfaction, his lack of curiosity. In his mind, OCD was a problem and medicine was a solution – nothing more complicated then measuring and cutting a two-by-four. As he hunched over his pad, diligently recording his notes and charting the coming week's treatment, there was something of the child about him – the little boy who'd mastered his chemistry set.

His single-minded faith in the power of antidepressants wasn't just a professional bias; it was also a personal fetish. At one point, he told me about a fantasy of his. *Do you remember Scrooge McDuck's vault?* he asked. *The one where he jumps off a diving board and swims in a sea of gold coins? Well, I would like the same thing, only the vault would be full of pills.* He leaned back, smiling, fingers tented. *I would do the backstroke,* he said, circling his arms up and away.

It wasn't often that he said things like this, but it was more than I might have liked. I began to feel like an addict, indulging my dealer's stupid stories and annoying eccentricities in order to get my fix. The difference, I suppose, was that I believed in this; I trusted that the medicine was actually useful, even if the man doling it out was a little cracked.

Despite – or perhaps because of – his enthusiasm for antidepressants, my doctor was decidedly opposed to drugs of any other sort. A few months into our relationship, I called and asked whether it would be safe to smoke pot while on medication. (I had smoked prior to beginning treatment, but I was worried about mixing the two.)

I expected either an outright no or – much less likely – a very qualified yes, so I was shocked when he refused to answer the question entirely. And he didn't simply refuse; his voice quickly rose, and he threatened to discontinue treatment if I persisted with my questions.

I felt sheepish and furious at the same time. No, I didn't think smoking pot was a fantastic idea, but I did feel entitled to answers about its effects from my healthcare provider. "I'm not saying I'm going to do it," I told him. "But you're my doctor, and I'm asking you a basic question about how my body works. You're supposed to answer those questions."

He cut me off, nearly shouting: "Okay Matt, we're finished. I won't be treating you anymore."

This was worrisome. I felt exhausted just thinking about trying to find a new psychiatrist, much less having to explain my whole story again. I backed down, promising that I wouldn't smoke and begging him to take me back. He agreed.

I felt shaky and kicked around. *How did a man who abused his authority this way even obtain a license?* I wondered. *And what about all the people in his care who were even less capable of standing up for themselves than I was?* And then it occurred to me: *I don't actually have to listen to this guy.* By overusing his professional power so blatantly, he had traded away his influence. *This man isn't particularly wise,* I thought. *He's just a supplier, and all I have to do is keep him happy.*

I called my other psychologist and explained what had happened. He didn't hide his professional dismay, and he agreed: there was nothing wrong with the questions I was asking. So, I asked, if I smoke pot on medication, am I going to damage my heart?

"I think if you have a puff, that should be okay."

A puff. How cute. Either this man wasn't familiar with pot (who uses that word? and who only has one 'puff'?) or he was trying to maintain a professional stance in the midst of a seamy conversation. I read between the lines: pot was basically fine. But like most healthcare providers, my psychologist was playing it conservative, and he didn't feel like he could say that out loud.

For the next several years, I drank and smoked pot regularly. Drinking had its place – it was fun and social and silly – but I loved marijuana. When I was high, my mind slowed down to what felt like exactly the right speed. There weren't any extra thoughts – there were just the thoughts I was having. And while I still felt things I didn't like, I didn't necessarily try to escape. Like everything else, unpleasant emotions felt interesting, deep, and worthy of attention. I was experiencing more true presence than I ever had.

Soon enough, though, OCD infiltrated my smoking sessions as well. I became increasingly focused on achieving a very particular mindstate, so I started monitoring my feelings with counterproductive precision. I didn't want to smoke too little; what was the point of getting a little buzzed when heavenly feelings and life-changing insights were another bowl away? And I didn't want to smoke too much, to whoosh right past high and into the dead, stoned space that came afterward; that was just burning neurons for nothing.

Along with my blooming rigidity, I remembered the phone call with my psychiatrist. Despite his outrageous behavior, I began to feel that he had been right. Not on the facts of the matter, exactly – we hadn't even discussed those – but on a moral and emotional level. My OCD was kicking into gear, capitalizing on my tendency to feel guilty about everything and creating one more rule for me to follow. If I wanted to be a good person – if I wanted the right to feel free of guilt – there'd be no smoking allowed.

But that didn't stop me. Instead, I just went round and round – smoking, maybe even enjoying myself, and then feeling anxious and ashamed for days or weeks afterward. I developed increasingly intense obsessions about the costs of smoking: *Would I start losing memories? Would I be able to process what I was reading in school as well as I had before? Was I trading away the one thing I had going for me – my intellectual horsepower – in the name of rapidly shortening bursts of escapist fun?* I began examining my mind's functioning for signs of decay; every thought contained an extra thought about why I wasn't thinking as well as I had before. Nights of smoking no longer stood alone; they now came with weeks of stupor and self-recrimination in train.

Then guilt infected the act of smoking itself. Instead of getting high and feeling the moral and emotional hangover afterward, I began to feel regret and fear as I rolled the joint, as I bought an eighth, as I thought about whether to smoke at all.

I could see that something wasn't working, that smoking no longer provided any distance from the self-cannibalizing tedium of my mind. On the other hand, I felt entitled to at least a little pleasure. Others had their beer, their wine – was this any different? More to the point, weren't my newfound fears exactly the kinds of things that had driven me to smoke in the first place?

Naturally, I didn't make any quick and decisive choices about how to handle the situation. Instead, I argued with myself for several more years – back and forth, back and forth, never making any headway or gaining any lasting insight. Until the stalemate broke.

I say "broke" in the passive voice, because I know it wasn't me doing the breaking. Instead, I simply reached a point where that trade-offs no longer seemed worth it – where depression and self-flagellation had so thoroughly colonized my experience that I didn't feel much temptation to smoke anymore. I still vacillated, of course, and if you can use the word 'relapse' about smoking marijuana, then I did that too. But eventually, the cycle wore itself out.

By the time I graduated college, I was taking 30 mg of Lexapro (a newer version of Celexa). This is the "therapeutic dose" for OCD, and it's where I've been ever since.

As I moved around, I found a new psychiatrist; when he retired, I began getting my prescriptions refilled through my GP. Neither of these men cared much for numbers or questionnaires. Instead, they seemed to treat medicine as a natural adjunct to my condition: *Oh, you have OCD? Well of course you'll be taking an SSRI.*

I've thought about working with these men to experiment with my dosage levels, or perhaps even trying a new medication entirely. But I've always held off. For the last six years, I've also been undergoing a form of cognitive behavioral therapy known as exposure and response prevention, and I've never wanted too many variables in the mix. (If I saw improvement, how would I know what had made the difference?)

More than that, though, the world of medication has always felt deeply murky to me. I've asked my doctors questions, of course. (*Why this medicine over that one? What are the potential trade-offs?*) But even when I ask good conceptual questions, there's still a communication gap. I don't know anything about neurochemistry, and I think my doctors feel that they have no choice but to summarize and simplify.

More than that, though, my psychiatrists haven't always agreed about dosage levels. I strongly suspect that this is because they haven't all had the same level of specialized training in the treatment of OCD. (As with medicine more generally, psychiatry has its niches, and it isn't particularly easy to find people well-trained in OCD.)

Of course, nothing is stopping me from diving into the scientific literature myself. But I've hesitated to do so – partly because I don't have the neurochemistry training that would help me interpret the research meaningfully, and partly because so much of it is new and inconclusive anyway.

At a more basic level, though, I find something repellent about the idea of second-guessing my psychiatrists. Not because I put them on a pedestal – I don't – but because the nature of OCD is to second-guess everything (and third-guess, and fourth-guess...). OCD creates an unending trust deficit, and one of the most useful things about treatment is the way it's helping me relearn to trust. Even if that trust is in some sense misplaced – perhaps there's a slightly more effective combination of medicine out there – it still feels valuable to orient myself this way. To place trust in trust itself.

When I wrote that last paragraph, it felt both true and incomplete. Yes, the aim of OCD treatment is to train in non-reactivity – to not indulge my mind's compulsive desire to revisit and relitigate everything all the time. To trust that my life isn't going to fall apart if I don't keep myself under 24-hour surveillance.

But that doesn't mean trusting naïvely, nor does it mean interpreting every one of my questions as compulsive.

And when it comes to my hesitation to learn more about antidepressants, there *is* something compulsive going on. It's an arena in which the stakes feel high, in which I feel pressure to get it right but no confidence in my ability to do so. In other words, a perfectly fertile breeding ground for new obsessions and compulsions.

OCD is a clever bastard. It makes me suffer, and then it tells me that there's no use trying to learn how not to suffer, because doing so will only lead me suffer more. In other words, that none of my impulses are trustworthy – that the only thing I can trust is that things will go on like this. But that is just classic totalitarian bullshit – the regime telling its citizens that no other reality is possible, and then making it a crime to think otherwise. In other words, curiosity isn't always compulsive. The world isn't already ruined. Things might just be okay.

That might sound like a rather meager cry for freedom, but if you know OCD, you'll know otherwise.

OCD AND THE COMPULSION
NOT TO COMPULSE

In therapy, I've learned that I have one job: not to compulse. No matter how much fear I feel, no matter how creative and tormenting my thoughts may be, I'm to resist the impulse to react and ritualize. I'm to stand on the beach as the typhoon bears down, as it comes ashore, as it breaks me against the dunes.

As you can imagine, I'm awfully tempted to do otherwise, to do whatever I can to escape the onrushing waves. But trying to avoid intrusive thoughts through compulsive behavior is like trying to escape the sun's heat by putting on more clothing: you buy yourself a moment's reprieve, but then things get much worse. Compulsions are closed loops, perpetual motion machines, self-cannibalizing Möbius strips. They feed on themselves, which is why it's so important to starve them of fuel.

Over the last several years, I've taken my therapist's instructions to heart. I spend hours each day trying to resist the temptation to wash my hands again, to reread that email, to review that conversation one more time. Perhaps predictably, then, I've developed a compulsion not to compulse.

Scientists tell us that it will never be possible to predict the weather more than thirty days in advance. Beyond a certain point, there's simply too much uncertainty in play.

If there is wisdom in meteorologists' restraint, I don't heed it. Instead,

I spend lots of time trying to predict and forestall, to spy around corners, to survey my territory from the sky. I want to catch compulsions in embryo, to pour water on the kindling.

And from a certain point of view, all of this decoding and counterintelligence work makes sense. After all, compulsions often appear in disguise – the friendly fruitseller hiding VC weapons. *Is my desire to finish reading this chapter a compulsive reflection of my generally type-A personality? Or is my impulse to stop reading itself a compulsion, born of a desire to avoid straining my eyes? And is the very fact that I'm now caught up in this debate another compulsion altogether, a product of my mind's insistence on perfect self-awareness and flawless decision-making?* This is the soundtrack of the rabbit hole.

It's also an unwinnable game. I feel the obligation to identify compulsions before they manifest, but I don't know what I'm looking for.

My therapist recommends a simple acid test: when I feel myself struggling, caught up in a fear-driven debate, then I'm likely on the verge of compulsing. And in those situations, I don't have to decide what's actually happening or try to divine the best course of action – I'm free to cut the tension and walk away.

But OCD has a way of coopting any gesture toward freedom back into servitude. The other morning, for example, I sat down to do a quick bit of email before leaving the house. I didn't want to get drawn into a long computer session; I'd been spending lots of time in front of the screen, and I needed to puncture the claustrophobia and get outside. So I made myself a little deal: just one email. But inevitably, the tempting opening lines of a second email pulled me in, and I found myself clicking.

To my surprise, I didn't want to finish reading it – I was tired and unable to focus. And in a flash, the first debate (should I open the email?) was entirely displaced by a second one (should I finish reading?).

OCD loves a debate – the more confusing, intractable, and nonsensical, the better. In this case, the debate quickly became several, all happening simultaneously. *Am I obligated to finish? No, of course not. (So long as you're not stopping out of a compulsive fear of the consequences if you do.) So am I allowed to finish? (Sure. Just as long as you're not doing so because you believe you're supposed to – so long as that's what you really want.) So should I stop? (Fine, so long as it's not because you fear that you'll hurt your eyes by continuing.) But aren't I allowed to walk away when I'm struggling? (Oh, is that what's happening here? Or are you so afraid of OCD that you imagine its presence even when it's not there?)*

This is the template, the boxing match that OCD is constantly promoting: *Is this against the rules, or do I just not want to do it?* Meanwhile, the words on the screen were getting blurry. And as the argument in my head intensified, the external world quietly receded. It didn't occur to me that anything existed outside this conversation.

LIFE IN A GLASS CAGE

AN EXTENDED METAPHOR FOR OCD

I magine you live in a glass box just slightly larger than your body. It is shaped such that you can neither sit nor stand. Through the glass, you see the world going to and fro. It looks very inviting, and you think, *If only I could crack the glass, I'd have my freedom.*

But another part of you knows that isn't true. You've tried many times before. Sometimes, you've pulled your body back as far as you could, then slammed forward. But the glass was far too thick, and you found yourself woozy and bleeding.

Other times, you've fractured the glass with a well-placed elbow, only to feel the panes spray inward, shocking your skin with their edges.

For a while, you learned helplessness. And then you began to wonder how you ended up in this cage to begin with. Who put you here, and why?

The construction is too precise, you notice, the seals flawless. There are no joints or nails or hinges – just one single unbroken pane, perfectly curved to accommodate your body. There is just enough air to keep you breathing and no more.

The case is an exoskeleton.

It is yours, a part of you like your toes or your hips or your earlobes. It is more so, actually, because you could do without these bits. But the glass cannot be dispensed with, because it is an outward projection of your mind. You've been sitting still for a very long time, afraid of what a twitch or gesture might bring. The glass is solid because you are. And you can learn to move.

OCD ABROAD

A few days ago, I published an essay that I'd been working on for several months. It had been a long and challenging process, and I'd felt a quiet excitement as the project wound its way to a natural conclusion. As soon as I hit 'publish,' though, the usual ego-oriented anxiety arose. I found myself craving reactions – checking Facebook for likes and shares, counting retweets, and hoping against hope for the golden ticket – commission requests from magazines.

Because I'd poured so much of myself into the essay, my anxiety was greater than usual. I'm on a brief vacation at the moment, but I had little interest in seeing the sights – I didn't want to be far from my computer, didn't want anyone to wonder why I wasn't responding more quickly to their comments. A few times, the anxiety became claustrophobic enough that I had to force myself into the streets and onto a moto-taxi. *Take me anywhere*, I thought, *but get me away from that tiny little room.*

Gravitational force is inversely proportional to the square of the distance between two objects; out among the pagodas, my computer's tractor beam was weak. Eventually, though, the heat or hunger would send me back indoors, and I would confront my computer once again – a smug little idol surveying its realm.

I would be casual at first – *Just a quick dip into email, no big deal.* Soon enough, though, my anxiety would take the form of the usual OCD schoolmarm. *Can you afford to wait a few days before responding to some of this feedback? Might waiting be a good thing, in fact? Might it even be the* best *thing? If so, then that's what you've got to do. So why are you still at the keyboard, asshole?*

None of my thoughts or feelings about the situation felt quite accurate, but that didn't make them any less persuasive. I'd feel fifty-one percent drawn in one direction, and I'd begin to move that way. Then the margin would start to feel flimsy – *What's one percent?* – and I'd find myself drifting back toward the ballast of the other, now-neglected forty-nine percent.

After ping-ponging for a while, I saw that I was stuck in the same old pattern, acting out a craving for assurances that my choices were right, true, and good. Usually, of course, such certainty isn't available, but that rarely occurs to me. Instead, I take on the situation's whole guilt-ridden burden; I believe that there *are* guarantees out there, and that I feel anxious because I'm too incompetent to find them.

And in this situation, that's exactly how things unfolded. My belief in my own asshole-ishness was like any other repressed idea – just out of visual range, but completely in control. I was a disaster of a human being, spoiled to the core.

Alongside this existential judgment came a more situation-specific one. Yes, I was a jerk – that much was a given. But I only felt this *much* anxiety because I was doing something wrong right then and there. And what was I doing wrong, exactly? Why, typing, of course. Yes – that must be the culprit. After all, I'd already begun to worry about the health of my hands, to wonder at the meaning of the little tweaks in my right ring finger. Now I'd 'discovered' that I'd been right to worry.

With this, my two worries converged. I felt anxious about responding to my readers' emails because I suspected that it might take more than my hands had to give, and I felt anxious about my hands because I was forcing them to serve my ego's need for validation. The loop was complete – asshole behavior, all around.

The circuit wasn't just mental. It was physical, too – I truly felt discomfort in my hands as I typed. But I also knew that the degree of distress I felt wasn't due to the pain alone. It was turned up to eleven by my confusion and suffering, to the point where I actually couldn't distinguish the two. I couldn't even locate the finger pain, exactly – it was larger than my fingers themselves, and it was visual, floating in a multi-colored haze somewhere between my head and my hands.

I vowed not to type for the rest of the day. Compulsive, perhaps, but it was pretty clear that I wasn't making any headway trying to figure out whether my impulses were sane. *Just walk away, Matt.*

As I sat in meditation later in the day, though, I saw just how much duress I'd been under when I'd made that pledge. *You were terrified, and you made a fearful decision. Nothing wrong with that, of course, but you're also not bound to stick with promises made under torture.*

As these thoughts flitted around behind my eyes, I felt the typing ban lift; when my meditation session was over, I returned to the computer. And for the next forty-five minutes, I was able to type more or less pain-free.

But reprieves are always only temporary. By the next day, I was caught in the same bitchy argument between fear and defiance. This time, though, I began to notice something else. It wasn't the typing that bothered me, exactly. It was *what* I typed. If I worked on this essay, for example, my mind gave me relatively little trouble. Clicking over into Facebook was much chancier, though. What began as innocent curiosity would quickly morph into something needier, graspier. I would find myself clicking down the rabbit hole, splashing and floundering through whirlpools of anxiety. As I did, the pain in my fingers would flare. I was beginning to see something: the pain wasn't 'real', exactly – it was guilt, manifesting in coercive and underhanded form.

For me, an insight like this is next to meaningless on its own. Instead, I have to have it dozens of times – often over many years – before it begins to sink in. And so the pattern continued over the next few days: anxiety, confusion, and pain would tag-team, pummeling me from all sides. I would respond with my behavioral therapy mantras, leaning into and agreeing with the fears. *Yup, you've fucked up your hands, and you're not going to be able to type anymore.* But I couldn't keep up the slightly ironic attitude that the therapy demands. Rather than inuring me to my fears, I was beginning to believe them even more deeply.

Sometimes, I'd give up entirely, resigning myself to my diminished fate. And right about then, something would loosen. After hours of being thrown around in the merciless surf, I'd be tossed up onto a spit of rock. I'd lay there, watching the ragged edges of my breath begin to soften. I'd notice my hands loosen and watch as my fists unclenched. I wasn't fighting anything. I was unwinding. It was a depressive relaxation, but it was relaxation nonetheless.

And then I'd head back to the computer, and the cycle would begin again.

Driving through the Cambodian night is not so different from driving through the night anywhere else, if you let it be. The gaunt cows like old men, acknowledging our bus as proof of that long-held truth: *buses come this way.* Kids, backlit on concrete porches, playing at karate. The rice fields, endless, and no less beautiful for their repetition.

Does anyone enjoy farming rice? I wonder. Do people still feel in tune with the season's rhythms, rising and resting with the sun? Or does wading through the rows begin to feel futile after a time? (The farmer's body ages, but the fields remain.) In a world of choices, would anyone choose this?

It's an absurd comparison, I know. Yet in some sense, I feel the same way about the laptop in my bag. This work – this blank screen. I rise each morning, stumbling toward it. This tiny plot of land dying to bear its fruit, if I can only learn the patience that its harvest requires. The bus approaches its terminal, and I hoist mine onto my back.

SUCH, SUCH WERE THE JOYS

OCD, ORWELL, AND JERKING OFF

I squeeze the brakes on my motorbike to come to a quick stop, and a brief pain slices through my fingers. *That's what happens when your mind wanders and you go too fast, asshole. You end up hurting yourself – exactly what you deserve.*

This is a core element of my religion: the belief that I should never end up in situations where I have to act erratically (and that doing so indicates a failure of foresight, a recklessness). *What did you care about more than preventing this? Probably something stupid, like a moment's thrill.*

My perfectionism wants me to be an expert at everything. Of course, it knows that this isn't quite possible, so it makes occasional concessions: I'm allowed to be a novice in some arena, so long as I approach that arena with the perfect mix of curiosity and beginner's prudence. It's the Goldilocks dilemma – no bowl is ever just right, which means I don't get to eat very often.

Which brings us to masturbation. For me, jerking off is a surgeon's theater for OCD – the perfect vantage point for watching intrusive thoughts and their accompanying compulsions snip and pierce and shave and section my mind into quivering little pieces. So, you know – pretty damn sexy.

There was a heyday at 13, of course. But not too long into my career, I realized – vaguely at first, then more clearly – that I often felt like I was chasing something. Finishing felt good, but treating the end as a goal felt inconsistent with the spontaneous sexiness that usually kicked things off.

Not that that stopped me. Like many of my friends, I was quickly hooked on porn. First came the magazine-and-VHS variety; two friends got into the habit of lifting Playboys from a mall bookstore, and I once followed suit. (Guilt quickly gobbled me up, so I returned to the store and dumped the magazine on the counter. Eighty-five percent of me was profoundly embarrassed, but the rest of me was more relieved than I'd known it was possible to be.)

Despite these tawdry episodes, there was an innocence about it all – I was just figuring out what my body could do, and apparently it could do some pretty amazing things. Perhaps because of the porn, though, that exploratory idyll didn't last very long. Instead, I quickly developed a series of ideas about what my body should be capable of. It was the standard stuff: I thought I was supposed to be able to get hard at a wind's whisper, come on command, and then repeat without delay. Even in the headiest days of pubescence, though, it doesn't always work that way. As a woman was to tell me years later, *There's such a thing as feeling sexy.*

These days, my motivation seems to be waning. There's the initial impulse, and I get all geared up for the old game. But often, the momentum fades. Conjuring images is more of an effort, and the whole thing feels absurd. Why bother? *Because it feels good,* says the loop tape. Does it? I occasionally feel like one of Kundera's old men, wanting to want things that I no longer want (or feeling like I'm supposed to – which is basically the same thing). All of which would be fine, except at this point I'm often taken over by tunnel vision. As with sex, it's orgasm or bust.

The tunnel is constructed of two fears – that I won't be able to escape my neurotic patterns, and that I'll fuck myself up if I don't. The argument begins with a threat: *If you stop this time, maybe you'll be more likely to peter out early* next time. The tunnel will get narrower and dingier, and it'll go on like that forever – until you reach the arid, sexless desert at the tunnel's end.

Out of this threat comes an exhortation to a twisted nobility: *If you* stop, you're going to feel cowardly – that you've been spooked into panic by your own compulsions. But that's only going to make the tunnel smaller and more claustrophobic. Courage, then! Jerking off becomes manning the barricades.

Eventually, though, the pendulum swings, and I acknowledge something else – that continuing feels compulsive too. You're addicted to these ideas about the meaning of orgasm, and addiction always hurts. (That's part of the reason you gave up porn!)

The Dalai Lama tells us that if we can fix a problem, we needn't worry about it. And if we can't fix it, well, we needn't worry about that either. Fine, I think – but which is it?! Do I quit or keep going?

And at around this point, a third feeling arises – a sense-certainty that this internal debate will never end. With this feeling comes a thought – that the pain I'm enduring is somehow perfectly appropriate. You're an addict, and this is an addict's fate. Descriptively, that feels true, but there's more going on – a deep judgment, a sense that I somehow deserve all of this.

Such thoughts are the children of madness, and the counter-evidence is everywhere. Most pertinently: after living with physical and mental addictions my whole life, I'm basically healthy – working limbs, good eyesight, stirrings down below. But you don't expect any of this to actually register, do you?

I show up to a party at a bar, but I can't find anyone. Am I just early? No – forty-five minutes late is plenty fashionable. The music is crazy-makingly loud, and I feel my nerves unfurling. What to do with myself? How to pass the time?

This is the perpetual dance. Always greedy for more time, always resentful of constrictions and obligations – and then, when I have time, wondering how to fill it.

But that's not quite right. At home, I'd be fine – I'd have books and a computer and podcasts and a chair for meditation. Here, I'm without resources. In particular, I'm without a sense for how long things will be like they are right now. Five minutes? 30? The bar is enormous – how will I know if anyone's arrived? I could check my phone every so often – but HOW often? And won't that quickly land me in a compulsive spiral?

I feel like I can put up with most things, so long as I have a general sense for how long they'll last. This, of course, is the first lesson any torturer learns: *keep 'em guessing.*

I pull out my phone to check my email. I have a phobia about using my phone for this purpose, and I've developed a rule against it. But at the moment, I can't remember why. Gmail begins to load, and my nerves splay from a different angle. *This is okay, I tell myself. Your hesitation is probably something compulsive. Just go ahead.*

But I still feel halved. I sense the g-forces, the old loop of discomfort and self-condemnation. And now I remember why I don't like checking email on my phone: because it takes so damn long. What's meant to be a reprieve from boredom becomes a stressor for precisely the reason that I pulled out my phone in the first place – because everything takes forever to load, and it's not clear how long forever will last.

By my dim lights, I've now made a mistake – *You shouldn't have given in to temptation, jackass* – and the usual consequence algorithm kicks in. *You've fucked up your fingers, and the night is now compromised. Oh, you'll probably get through it, but all your efforts to enjoy yourself and connect with others will be undermined by your mind's slow decomposition.*

In other words: *You knew better, once. And once is all you should ever need.*

"Such, Such Were the Joys" is George Orwell's essay about a childhood spent in the cruel bosom of an early-twentieth-century English boarding school. Among other torments, the headmasters of Orwell's school enjoyed mocking him for his family's relative penury. He had no right to be treated like the wealthier children, they informed him, and if not for the headmasters' own large-heartedness, he would have had it much worse.

> To grasp the effect of this kind of thing on a child of ten or twelve, one has to remember that the child has little sense of proportion or probability. A child may be a mass of egoism and rebelliousness, but it has not accumulated experience to give it confidence in its own judgments. On the whole it will accept

what it is told, and it will believe in the most fantastic way in the knowledge and power of the adults surrounding it.

I have long since joined the dubious ranks of adulthood, but one group of authority figures continues to hold sway over me. These are my intrusive thoughts. They are my conquerors and my caretakers, a brutish judge and jury possessed of unanswerable power. I have spent a lifetime under their rule, a sequence of days that often end in exhaustion.

On this particular day, I wander out of the bar, craving nothing more than rest. I pocket my phone, squeeze into a tiny plastic chair by the roadside, and watch the kaleidoscope of nonsense in my mind. I idly consider going home. *I'm here, aren't I? I came out, gave it a college try – isn't that good enough?* Several minutes pass, and I'm paralyzed with confusion. I don't know any of the things I need to know – how to sit, where to put my hands, what to do with these thoughts.

On a whim, I check my phone again. People have arrived. I rise to find them.

THOUGHTS ON OCD AND SUICIDE

There are two reasons I've never thought seriously about suicide. The first is that I've never been in quite enough pain – I always believe, at some level, that the fever will break. But the second is that killing myself would wreck my parents.

It wouldn't even take suicide. My mom has long told me that if anything were to happen to me, she'd "be a basket case." Knowing this (or believing it, anyway) has made it impossible for me to turn and face suicide – and death more generally – squarely. I don't feel like suicide is an option, morally speaking, and that's always made me a little resentful. I learned self-condemnation at the feet of my mother – herself a victim of these dark arts – but the thought of trying to escape the cycle only intensifies it further. Suicide is one more rule that I'm not allowed to break.

This, of course, is how OCD works day-to-day. I suffer nearly constant fears of one kind or another. In an effort to keep my intrusive thoughts at bay, I'm forever imposing new statutes on myself. *(The last time you typed without your wrist guards, you felt some pain in your right ring finger and worried about it all day. No more typing without wrist guards, then – not even a quick email!)* 'No' becomes my watchword, 'yes' a sign of self-defeating recklessness. I stuff my life into smaller and smaller spaces to try to escape the enveloping stench of pain. In doing so, though, I trade the miasma for thinner and thinner air.

Suicide is the logical extension of this approach, the infinite finitude at the end of the path. It's also perfectly counter-productive, like realizing that I've painted myself into a corner and then erasing myself entirely. In other words, it feels short-sighted, and therefore self-indulgent and melodramatic. (I don't mean in general, of course. Who can know what other people suffer?)

Still, I've often been afraid that I'll do it – that some impish impulse will steer the wheel into the oncoming semi. It's a common fear, but, in my case, an unrealistic one. After all, I don't have strong urges to hurt myself, and I have no real history of self-harm. To be more precise: I've hurt myself, but only inadvertently, and only in the confusion of OCD-driven reactivity. During my sophomore year of college, for example, I was overwhelmed at the prospect of damaging my eyes, and I did everything I could to ensure that nothing touched them. Sometimes, though, I became so sick of my own vigilance that I would rub them feverishly, discharging the built-up anxiety in dozens of tiny revolutions (and in doing so, creating floaters in my vision and even more anxiety).

Regardless of how bad I feel, then, death holds no appeal – something in me wants to live. But this doesn't entirely soothe my nerves. Riding around on my motorbike, I sometimes become afraid that I've detected a slight jitter in my hands. Ruthless worries scale the walls: will the imp act up before I have a chance to stop it? (Does this happen to people – that they get it wrong, that they leap off buildings and find themselves surprised as they're falling?)

This isn't how the imp works, of course. It's just a thought, not a mugger with chloroform. But I'm afraid anyway.

I want to continue living, but I'm not sure I can say what I'm living *for*. There are some things I'd love to experience – publishing a book and going on a book tour, relating with those who share these experiences and expressing them to those who don't. Finding a long-term partner, each of us making the world less lonely for the other.

If I died without ever knowing these things, I think there'd be a sadness, a sense of unfulfilled potential. But I don't quite think of them as goals or make-or-break features of a well-lived life. Things just seem to move along, and living longer is simply more motion; I suspect that the stillness at the end will feel arbitrary and nonsensical *whenever* it happens. But perhaps that's because I'm still young and can't fully fathom the naturalness of slowing down.

I only began to love Márquez's *One Hundred Years of Solitude* when the characters began to die. It wasn't just that I wanted to finish the novel, and it certainly wasn't that I didn't like them. It's that their lives only began to take shape and make sense to me in retrospect – as the arc became clear, as it stopped being just one fucking crazy thing after another.

I skimmed past Márquez's magic. I wasn't interested in the gypsies' flying carpets or the general with seventeen sons or the lover who's accompanied by butterflies. I just wanted normal shit. And in the end, the characters' deaths – perhaps all deaths – are just that. As fantastical as the circumstances may be, there's something more basic at play – a moment of reckoning, a mirror reflecting everything that's come before and lending each life its singularity.

Right now, the prospect of dying feels random and absurd; when I imagine it, a pointless feeling settles over all the suffering I've experienced. But if death were to step out of its fearsome garments and become real – if I were to receive a terminal diagnosis, say – I'm not sure it would actually feel like that at all. I suspect that the feeling of pointlessness would disappear, and that things would line up – that there'd be a sense (if not a rationale) to things. That the end would create – and complete – the arc. It was like this, I might say. What other words would do?

AS LONG AS SOMETHING'S RUINED, WE'RE OKAY

THE OBSESSIVE-COMPULSIVE STYLE
IN AMERICAN POLITICS

The contemporary Tibetan meditation teacher Chögyam Trungpa Rinpoche described how we depend on our anxieties, fixations, and worries. However painful they may be, he suggested, they also serve as occupations – ways to stay busy, to keep moving, to avoid acknowledging some of the deeper truths about our lives.

I'd been studying CTR's teachings for about 18 months when this line of thinking stopped making sense to me. Until that point, I'd bought in fully to Buddhist notions of emptiness and groundless (at least insofar as one can understand and assent to these things intellectually). I no longer believed that "I" was a coherent entity, and I wanted to see underneath the hood – to perceive more of the roiling energies and contradictory impulses sloshing around my mind.

My obsessions and compulsions also no longer felt like they were masking anything else. It all just felt like pain, and pain of a particularly useless sort. I would have happily given it up, even if it meant more existentially unsettling confrontations with whatever lay beneath – but I couldn't figure out how.

I asked my meditation teacher about this. She didn't say much, but I got the sense that she thought I was approaching the problem superficially. Sure, I would happily trade away my obsessions and fixations at any given moment – who wouldn't? But at a more basic level, she suggested,

I depend on my obsessive-compulsive patterns. They're my way of orienting myself, of understanding myself and the world around me. Living with OCD means inhabiting a shittily pessimistic perspective, true – but it's still a perspective, a point of view, a place to stand. Something is always wrong, or about to be. It's the perfect interpretive alloy, adaptable to any situation but fundamentally solid.

Our politics depends on the same psychology: a profound desire for certainty, and an equally profound pessimism about the prospect of finding it.

Take the frenzy with which we cut the world into simple pieces. In the US, there are (basically) two political parties, and these parties tussle over a relatively small number of 'issues.' Every player in the game receives a label – "progressive," "conservative," "radical" – that is meant to define his or her relationship to these 'issues.' Players rely on 'positions' (however recently and expediently chosen) and oppositions (however false) in order to convey a sense that they are in possession of the good and the true. The game itself is fundamentally adversarial and winner-take-all. There is almost no room for nuance or complexity. We need so badly to be right – about something, about *anything* – that we argue over the most trivial bullshit on Sunday morning talk shows.

And it's this need for certainty that gives rise to our pessimism. We *have* to be right; our guys *have* to get elected. If they don't, the world will fall apart. Our drive for certainty becomes a self-confirming loop. We're right, because we can't countenance the possibility of being wrong, nor the prospect of living in a world where truth is elusive. Watch the faces of the TV talking heads; behind their anger, you'll see terror.

In *The Paranoid Style in American Politics*, Richard Hofstadter writes, "We are all sufferers from history, but the paranoid is a double sufferer, since he is afflicted not only by the real world, with the rest of us, but by his fantasies as well."

Hofstadter is right, but he doesn't go far enough. In our drive for certainty, we are all paranoids, we are all fantasists. To say it differently, we are all obsessive-compulsives, driven by intrusive fears to build (and hide inside) elaborate philosophical fairylands.

Ultimately, though, it doesn't matter how badly we need certainty, because the world doesn't respond to our tantrums or pleas. However tightly we wrap ourselves in the mantle of ideology, however fervently we devote ourselves to this or that leader, however passionately we seek to demonstrate the logical consistency of our ideas, something in us knows that we're fooling ourselves. And it's this something – call it intelligence, call it intuition – that is the only thing really worth listening to.

WHAT I'M TRYING TO LEARN TO SAY

When friends ask how I'm doing, I often tell them that I've been "struggling with OCD stuff." There was a time when this was hard to acknowledge, and doing so brought relief – even a bit of pride. These days, though, "OCD stuff" doesn't feel specific enough. I want to do more than gesture in the direction of my struggles.

When I try to shade in the outlines, my first instinct is to specify what I've been worrying *about* (hands, eyes, knees, balls, whatever). Again, this felt useful for a time – a way to provide my listener a glimpse into the cauldron without too much risk that I'd fall in. Anymore, though, this tack doesn't provide much traction. After all, the worries are always *somewhere*.

That's not to say that eye-related worries feel exactly the same as teeth-related worries, of course. Each anxiety projects a distinct future; imagining blindness feels very different than imagining being unable to write. Still, there is a constant feeling underlying all of these neuroses – a crouchy, mingy way of seeing myself and the world. And this is what I want to talk about. It isn't really a matter of which number came up on the roulette wheel today. It's what it feels like to be trapped in this petty, unwinnable game.

TWELVE FRAGMENTS

0

First Movers. The universe was created, or it has always existed. We have no justification for believing one over the other.

1

Speed's Oblivion. I lived in Hanoi for a while, bumping around town on my motorbike, sidecar full of worries. Around Hoan Kiem Lake, I would merge into the whizzy traffic, hungry for speed's oblivion. I crashed twice; was this my good fortune?

2

The Meaning of Pain. I badly want the freedom to get things wrong, to feel like mistakes aren't always followed by consequences. Just now, I sat down to dinner. The fish was too hot, but I ate it anyway. I wanted to screw up, to scald the roof of my mouth, to experience discomfort as a transient state rather than a down payment on endless punishment. To believe that experiencing pain doesn't prove that I'm irredeemably flawed.

3

The Aftermath. I've been through countless little hurricanes at this point – hours or days or weeks when I'm picked up by the winds and thrown through walls. The impact leaves me speechless, a husk amidst the scattered trash. Like water, my mind seeks its lowest level – dark, quiet, stillness. I lay prone in bed, covers pulled, white flag flapping.

After an uncertain interval, the winds retreat, and my body picks up on the pressure changes. Itchy energy returns to my limbs, non-traumatized thoughts to my mind. I rise and walk outside – for an ice cream, perhaps, or just to remind myself that the rest of the world exists. At a certain point, I'm more-or-less out the other end, wobbly but recovering. I feel my feet advancing, one after the other. No tremors rumble, no chasms open. I'm braced by trustworthy streets and bobbleheaded children.

I'm also left with the feeling that nothing happened.

And in a sense, nothing did. I felt a bunch of fear, and my mind generated a heap of terrible thoughts to match the underlying emotion. In other words, my brain short-circuited, and then it invented a backstory to explain why. There was no *there* there – only panic.

But often, I only feel this kind of sobriety after the storm winds have settled down. In the moment, things are much too vivid for that; it's very hard to doubt the waves as they crash down on you. Even if it was, as we say, 'all in my head,' I still went through something – and I want explanations. *I'm bloodied and shaking here – something must have caused this.*

4

The Event. The proper study of history is about much more than identifying the causes that lead to events. It is about asking what *constitutes* an event. The things most people wouldn't notice and certainly wouldn't think twice about – a twitch here, a twinge there – are the things OCD wants to think about *forever*. OCD is a 30's newsboy shouting from streetcorners, a melodramatic newsanchor interrupting my regularly scheduled programming to bring me an important announcement. *Something has happened here,* it says. *And it's a big fucking deal.* Behind the teleprompter, OCD types its shitty revisionist history.

I find myself plunging backward, sifting through fragments of memory, trying to track down the first instance of suffering. *Was it when I lifted the pencil with two fingers rather than three? Or was it earlier – perhaps last night, when I stayed up too late and left myself exhausted, unable to respond to these thoughts skillfully?* This, too, is part of OCD's game – the obsession with the moment when life went wrong, the second before the Fall. And as with Eden, it's a set-up. *Here's a tree full of super-tempting fruit! But don't eat any of it. Why not, you ask? Oh, no reason – except that I am a petty, small-minded god, and I will hurt you very badly if you do.*

5

To Switch Metaphors. I want to understand why the rock rolled down the hill so I don't have to keep pushing it back up. But there's no such thing as science here. As I scrutinize the rock, as I replay its endless downward tumble, I find myself bumping downhill as well.

6

Why So Seductive, Then? It's partly the unpredictability of OCD experience that leaves me so stupefied, like a rat jolted with electricity at random. It would be easy to learn helplessness here, to retreat from all the places I've been shocked and skitter into the smallest corner of the cage. And I've often done exactly that.

Other times, though, I see the claustrophobia coming, and I find myself asking questions instead. *Where is this coming from? What triggered it? Why now? And when will it come next?* It's tempting to believe that answering these questions will provide me the resources I need to respond better next time, but usually this isn't so. Instead, it's an invitation to re-create the trauma, to etch it more deeply in stone.

7

The Unattractiveness of the Past. Thinking about the past rarely leads me anywhere good. There are images that stand undiluted, of course – scenes, faces, feelings. But if I gaze at them for any length of time – or if I scan forward or backward for even a second or two – I detect the anxiety that's shot through it all. I watch from the volcano's rim for a moment, and then I find myself sliding down into the red. Old fears bubble out of dormancy, new ones shudder and flash, and I no longer remember what it feels like to be anywhere else.

8

What's at Stake Here? I regret that things weren't different, but regret's metaphysics make no sense. Regret becomes lament, but lament throws good money after bad. Lament morphs into grief – a sadness for that tortured boy, and a sadness that I can't stop thinking about him.

9

The Future's No Better. OCD's greed isn't satisfied with the past. It demands the future, too, assuring me that things will never be much different than they are now. Or, rather, that they'll never be better, but that they could be much worse. *It's up to you,* OCD whispers. *How badly do you want to avert the suffering that's barreling your way?*

10

All of This Happens in the Present. (Where else can things happen?) But feeling things in the present and *being* in the present are very different matters. OCD only permits the former. *Sure, you can feel things, but those feelings will always refer you back to the sins of your past or reveal glimpses of your coming ruination. Yours will be a starved and desiccated present, the furthest thing from a gift.*

11

Another Kind of Present. It's possible to live in a present that doesn't make reference to past or future. That interprets the brain's flares as nothing more than signals sent by drunken sailors. That watches their fiery arc, their trailing smoke, their fading and disappearance into a murky sky.

I've seen this; I've known it, if only for moments.

THE MYTH OF SELF-INFLICTED SUFFERING

A QUICK CONVERSATION WITH MYSELF

For me, the hardest thing about OCD is the sense that I'm doing this to myself – that it's my fault that I just spent five hours thinking about whether I subtly (and almost painlessly) fractured my pinky finger. That all of that nausea, despair, and loneliness was self-inflicted.

Wasn't it?

Well, any sophisticated psychology would ask, What's this 'self' we're talking about?

Sure, sure. There's no self, no soul, no solid entity at our core. So maybe when we say 'self-inflicted,' we're really just saying that there's no Other, no one else to blame.

Right – but once we acknowledge that fluidity and interdependence are basic features of our existence, this whole self/other distinction starts to break down.

Not entirely. Even if there's no 'thing' inside me, there is a difference between what's happening here and what's happening elsewhere. My thoughts and feelings are still distinct from yours. In more Buddhist terms: karma operates locally. And so does consciousness.

So when we say that suffering is 'self-inflicted,' all we really mean is that it arises from within my thoughts and feelings. Which leads to the question - how could suffering be anything *other* than self-inflicted?

It couldn't. Without thoughts and feelings – without consciousness – there would be no suffering.

So why am I so irked by this phrase?

Because it suggests that there is someone to blame, *and that someone is me (or a part of me). But once we see that we aren't coherent, self-controlling entities – that the mind itself is a braid made up of different patterns of thought, feeling, and perception – then there isn't anyone there to inflict the suffering, and there isn't anyone to inflict it on. Stuff's just happening.*

Sounds kind of fatalistic.

At a deep level, yes. (No free will, etc.) But most of the time, we don't live our lives at that level, and there's no need to. We can just look at what's happening in our minds and ask whether it's worth listening to.

As you said, though, our minds aren't one thing – they're composed of many parts. So who's doing the looking and listening? When we 'look at what's happening in our minds,' all we really mean is that one part is responding to another. Sometimes these parts respond with care and love, but other times – as with OCD – they can be nasty and cruel.

Yes! The parts of my mind that OCD has commandeered are profoundly nasty – tyrants and bullies bent on crushing the other, more vulnerable parts.

Interesting – you're implying that OCD itself is only part of your mind. Often, though, you talk about your mind as if it were one big OCD-infested junkyard – you've used phrases like "broken brain" in your essays. But of course, if your mind were nothing but OCD, then you wouldn't be vulnerable. (You wouldn't have any self-awareness, either, but perhaps you'd be pain-free.) It's only because OCD attacks the tender parts of your mind that you feel a contrast – and that you suffer.

Right again! And maybe that's how it makes sense to talk about a 'self' – as the collection of all of these parts. OCD is a virus, forever trying to pervade and infect every other aspect of my being. But regardless of whether it's got the upper hand on any given day, it's still only part of me, and never the whole. Which means that it probably doesn't make sense to identify with it as much as I have.

That might be another reason to reject the phrase 'self-inflicted' – because it can imply that what's happening is coming from all of me (or the 'truest' or 'deepest' parts). But it isn't – it's only coming from the part that's most powerful *right now*. There are other parts, too, and they each need to be heard.

ON THE VIRTUE OF

SPINELESSNESS

At the conclusion of *A Song Flung Up to Heaven*, Maya Angelou describes how black people have survived four hundred years of slavery and oppression in America.

> I thought of human beings, as far back as I had read, of our deeds and didoes. According to some scientists, we were born to forever crawl in swamps, but for some not yet explained reason, we decided to stand erect and, despite gravity's pull and push, to remain standing.

A few pages later, I finished what seemed like the book's final chapter. I couldn't be sure, though; my Kindle provides no page numbers. *Trust yourself – you know what the end of a book feels like.* I put the book down, then picked it back up. *It had progressed – and ended – oddly; perhaps Angelou had added a short coda? Nothing wrong with taking a quick look-see.*

As soon as I checked, (she hadn't) I found myself tumbling down the familiar slope. *You couldn't resist, could you? You're just so terrified of missing something, of failing to cross your t's, that you never let yourself actually experience anything – including the ends of things.*

Rest. Rest. I decided to lay down on the cafe's couch. As I took my glasses off, though, old fears about stabbing myself in the eyes burst to life. *Had I felt something at the corners of my eyes as my glasses' frame slid forward?* I laid my head down, and new thoughts took the floor: *was the pillow now pulling at my newly damaged eyes?*

This wasn't subtle, nuanced irony – it was the stuff of teenage melodrama, the Blue Angels over the Rose Bowl. Maya had just gotten finished telling me that it was the resolve to survive, to stand – firm-footed, straight-backed, and dignified – which had enabled black people to

> [r]ise out of physical pain and the psychological cruelties. Rise from being victims...to the determination to be no victim of any kind. Rise and be prepared to move on and ever on.

– and sixty seconds later, I was prone, then fetal. Forget dignity, forget determination; I couldn't even stand up.

Twenty minutes later, as I sat in meditation, the floodwaters began to recede. I found myself calmer, less claustrophobic. And it occurred to me: maybe a call to straight backs is exactly what some people (and peoples) require. For me, though, an insistence on determination – an insistence on *anything*, really – always ends up double-edged and curling inward. OCD demands perpetual warriorship, and threatens total disaster if I ever let my guard down. In other words, resistance may be part of the solution – but it's also the source of the problem.

Perhaps the analogy only goes so far. There are a hundred differences between the suffering Angelou describes and the kind generated by OCD, most of them too obvious to mention.

On the question of resistance, though, maybe the two aren't quite as distinct as I've suggested. There've been plenty of moments in my own treatment when I've sought to cultivate my resolve, to resist the temptation to indulge in fear-driven compulsions – to stand, feet planted, as the wind swirls.

The trouble starts when my resolve begins to weaken. I can lower my shoulder and redouble my efforts, sure, but eventually, I run out of fuel. And in those moments, I feel like I've failed myself – that my spine has bent to the breaking point, that my determination to be determined has proved inadequate. My demands of myself – and my inability to meet them – become the cords and fibers of a form-fitting net, and I find myself hoisted aloft and dangling.

In the waters below, I notice a jellyfish – that archetype of spinelessness. The jellyfish floats along, allowing the waves to surge through him. He suspects that the waters will subside at some point, but he doesn't fight the tide. He knows, after all, that he doesn't control the wind.

From my net, I shout to a friend. "See? The jellyfish!" I want to climb down, to float alongside him.

My friend's reply comes quickly: the jellyfish doesn't actually know he's floating. He doesn't know that he isn't resisting things. He doesn't know anything at all. We, on the other hand, are blessed and cursed with consciousness. "A standing human will never be a floating jellyfish," my friend reminds me, "because he is more aware of his standing than the jellyfish is of his floating."

I've been struggling with my net – trying to widen the holes, to squeeze my limbs between the twine. Her words land, and for a moment, I cease.

For us, floating means more than just relaxing our muscles and surrendering control. It means saying yes to *everything*, including our impulses to say no. It means feeling a thousand urges to fight – and sometimes actually fighting. Perhaps most often, it means not knowing whether to fight, flee, or bury our swords – and saying yes to that, too.

We do all of these things at the iceberg-tip of things, amidst the waves' splash and parry and unbearable self-importance. No matter how confused we may feel, though, we never really get it wrong. Instead, we are held up by the slow-moving and barely palpable currents of the deep. Fighting, too, is a form of floating.

UNSOLICITED ADVICE

OCD isn't complicated.

That probably sounds strange, given that I've just devoted a whole book to some of the many facets of this fucker. But it isn't – it's actually fairly straightforward. Your brain misfires, which sends a bad signal to your mind. You get uncomfortable, and you want to take action to make yourself feel better. But you can't, because that'll only make things worse.

Pretty simple, really. Murderously difficult to deal with, yes, but simple nonetheless – like a Chinese finger trap.

And if your brain is wired like mine, that's disappointing. Because I want this knot to be Gordian. I want this monster to be multi-legged and many-winged. I want the romance of fighting an elusive, shape-shifting enemy.

But there isn't much romance in OCD treatment. You get your sleep. You do your exposure exercises. And you resist the temptation to compulse. It's like AA – you just work the program. It's the soul's equivalent of bad coffee in church basements.

But when you're in that basement – all by yourself if you must be, with a friend if you can be – you realize that you don't give a shit about the way the coffee tastes. You're here because you have to be, because your life has brought you here, because everywhere else is just you running away from this work.

If you do the work, your life gets better. Maybe a little better, maybe a lot better, but better. If you don't, well – you know what that's like already.

But whatever you find yourself doing – and I mean this – don't judge yourself. And if you find yourself judging, don't judge that. OCD has abused you for years, and the last thing you need is to pile on more self-hatred. Instead, ask, "What's the most loving thing I can do for myself?" And then listen.

ACKNOWLEDGEMENTS

Josh, Dan, Bob, Andy, Mitz, Jay, Brianna, Riley, Teddy, Rob, Jenna,
Lee, John, Jesse, Mel, Will, Alex, Dr. Bailey, Dr. Maher, Mom, Dad, and
Nhung

WHAT WORDS?

———————

ABOUT THE AUTHOR

Matt Bieber is a freelance writer based in Ho Chi Minh City, Vietnam.
His work has appeared in *The Believer, Aeon, Shambhala Sun, The Dallas
Morning News*, and elsewhere. His second book, co-authored with Timothy
Patrick McCarthy, will be released in 2016.

Matt blogs and podcasts at mattbieber.net

Made in the USA
San Bernardino, CA
26 July 2016